COACH DEAN EOANNOU

The "Buffalo System" of Building Champions was created and developed by Coach Dean Eoannou. Coach Dean's boxers (6 women/18 men) have won 43 championships and medals including: 2 US National Golden Gloves Championships, Ringside World Championship, Ringside Masters World Championship and numerous Golden Gloves Championships. Coach Eoannou is certified by USA Boxing, inducted into the HALL OF FAME in 2018 Buffalo Veteran Boxers Association–Ring 44. www.parkinsonsboxing.com

DR. EUGENE B. KERN

Eugene "Doc" Kern, MD trained at Mayo Clinic in Minnesota as a surgeon and then served 2 years as a major in the US Air Force from 1968-1970. Dr. Kern was Professor of Rhinology and Facial Plastic Surgery at Mayo Clinic for 33 years and currently teaches Nasal, Sinus and Facial Surgery at UB in the Department of Ear Nose and Throat.

MARC MURPHY

Marc has been a commercial photographer since 1977 specializing in architecture, people and digital retouch. His work can be viewed at: www.murphyphoto.com

STEVEN KEOUGH

Steven is a technical patent writer with a strong love of sports. A graduate of the United States Naval Academy, Catholic University of America, Boston College Law School and a retired Navy Captain. His interest in boxing goes back to Annapolis, where he learned the basics in the martial arts as part of his overall military training.

Boxing: Essential Skills

Dean Eoannou

Head Coach, (UB) Boxing Club
State University of New York at Buffalo (UB)

Eugene B. Kern, MD

Emeritus Professor Rhinology and Facial Plastic Surgery
Department of Otorhinolaryngology Mayo Clinic
Professor of Otorhinolaryngology
State University of New York at Buffalo (UB)

The ***"Buffalo System"*** of Building Champions was created and developed by Head Coach Dean Eoannou. Coach Dean's boxers have won 43 Championships and medals (24 Champions: 6 women and 18 men) in 11 years. Page 131.

Three of Coach's boxers Wendy Casey (2008, 2017), Kristin Mc Murtree (2016) and Tim Akeredolu (2015) were voted Amateur Boxer of the Year by Buffalo Veteran Boxers Association–Ring 44
Updated: August 2018

EDITOR'S NOTE
Boxing: Essential Skills DVDs sold separately at boxingessentialskills.com

PREFACE

A funny thing happened on the way to my math degree, I became a New York State Golden Gloves boxing champion….and I got my math degree. Interestingly math and the "sweet science" of boxing are really connected! My coach, Dean Eoannou of the State University of New York at Buffalo (UB) Boxing Club, explained this connection to me. Essentially, boxing is all about motion (transferring your body weight) and delivering FORCE. And FORCE, according to Isaac Newton's second law of motion is equal to mass (your body weight) times acceleration (speed of your punch), or F=MA. The FORCE of your punch is the product of your total body weight multiplied by the speed at which you're able to punch.

Coach Dean explained that since my body weighed more than any man's arm, and that my legs were stronger than a man's arm, he could teach me how to transfer every ounce I weighed with every punch I threw. Coach taught me to transfer my body weight and explosively driving my punches through my legs producing a powerful forceful punch. Coach Dean promised using his "Buffalo System" I would be able to hit harder than any man who wasn't a trained boxer. It turned out to be true. Almost every punch I landed, and there were many, carried the full force of my body weight behind it.

The style of boxing in this book will help you become a hard-hitting explosive boxer, along with good footwork and great defense. If you want to become an amateur boxer, I advise four main things:

1. Read this book and watch the 2 DVDs which explains and teaches you the fundamentals of boxing, lesson by lesson, using New York State Golden Glove Champions, including me, who were trained by Coach Dean at the UB Boxing Club.
2. Learn to stay over your back foot when learning the essential foot work so you can learn to transfer all of your body weight with every explosive punch you throw.
3. Learn to use angles, which Coach Dean drums into your head, so you can be in position to hit your opponent without be hit in return.
4. Lastly, keep your hands up and your head moving so you can stay pretty, like me.
   The "Buffalo System" worked for me and it can work for you; teaching you the essentials of how to box and it can even prepare you to compete for a boxing championship, if you wish.
   I had no prior boxing experience; however, after learning the "Buffalo System" taught by Coach Dean. I won numerous boxing honors along with many members in the UB Boxing Club.
   New York State Golden Gloves Champion (Three times)
   New York State Empire Games Champion (Two times)
   New York State Empire Games Silver Medalist
   National Golden Gloves Bronze Medalist
   National Golden Gloves Silver Medalist
   Northeast Champion
   Amateur Boxer of the Year 2008,
   Buffalo Veteran Boxer's Association Ring 44
   (By unanimous vote and the first female ever to receive the award)

Keep your hands up, your head moving and come out punching, hard;
it's a great amateur sport!
Wendy Casey
Buffalo, New York
July 2014

Wendy Casey with Coach Dean Eoannou

DEDICATION

TO OUR FAMILIES
For their support.

TO OUR TEACHERS
For their wisdom.

TO OUR BOXERS
For their TRUST.

The Authors

July 2014

2nd Edition
September 2018

Table Of Contents

Table Of Contents

Table Of Contents

Table Of Contents

Table Of Contents

Table Of Contents

Table Of Contents

Introduction

Would you like to learn how to box? If the answer is yes, then this book is for you, the beginner (the novice). The book's primary purpose is simply the teaching of essential boxing skills to men and women interested in learning the amateur sport of boxing. Boxing is learned. There are no naturals. The book, photographs and companion TWO DVDs (VIDEO CLIPS) are designed for teaching the essential boxing skills (footwork and punches) to both Right-Handed and Left-Handed ("south paw") aspiring boxers.

Since this is a book for beginners, only the essentials are taught, which includes footwork movements, offensive punching including the first 3 punches, the first 2-punch combinations, defensive blocks and counter punches plus the 3 essential angles needed to avoid being hit. By mastering all the lessons in this book and on the TWO DVDs (**VIDEO CLIPS**) and we mean mastering ALL the lessons including physical conditioning, "Ring Drills", sparring and SKILLS TESTS (which are listed in PART 13: BOXING PERFORMANCE TESTS which MUST be passed and overseen by your COACH). These are the essential building blocks for becoming an accomplished boxer. THEN, AND ONLY THEN will you be prepared to comfortably proceed to the next level of learning, which is beyond the scope of this book. The next level includes 6 additional punches, more advanced ring skills and more intense conditioning required for competition so some day you WILL be prepared to compete for a CHAMPIONSHIP.

It usually takes 3 to 6 months of conditioning and skills training before you are ready for the "Ring Drills" and the sparring lessons in this book and contained on the TWO DVDs (**VIDEO CLIPS**). "Ring Drills" offer the opportunity to enter the ring with an experienced boxer who helps to "teach not injure" so you can improve and polish your skills on offense and begin to learn defense in the ring under the watchful eyes of your coach. After learning offense and defense during the "Ring Drills", you can begin the process of sparring in the ring with an experienced boxer so you can master the remaining essential lessons and skills for the beginner without being injured.

"Ring Drills" on DVD 1   VIDEO are exclusively for a Right-Handed boxer.
"Ring Drills" on DVD 2   VIDEO are exclusively for a Left-Handed boxer.

The DVD icons inform you, the reader, that a companion **VIDEO CLIP** is available for study. Eventually you must perform each building block without thinking, almost as a reflex. Mastering each skill and "Ring Drill" to perfection is your GOAL. Mastering these skills and "Ring Drills" requires many thousands of repetitions--so practice, practice and more practice over that 3 to 6-month period, which allows you to develop superlative footwork and powerful punching skills. These lessons and drills are building blocks where each lesson and drill progresses from the skills taught in the previous lesson. CAUTION: Do not proceed to the next lesson before you master the previous lesson; otherwise, you are building a flawed boxer. The progressive building block approach to learning how to box presented in this book has been successful at the University at Buffalo Boxing Club where both women and men have won numerous regional and state Golden Gloves Championships and national medals for boxing. Many of our champions were not high school athletes but determined students dedicated to learning how to box.

In our experience, we found that after learning to box, the individuals, both men and women, develop a new level of assuredness, which frequently infuses a new level of self confidence that extends to other areas of life and stays with you for the rest of your life. Boxing is NOT about punching or "beating someone up". Boxing is more than that. It is about passion, excitement for life, discipline, determination (heart), courage, integrity, character, humility, confidence, and respect--respect for your coaches, your daily practice sessions, your teammates, your opponents, the officials, the sport and sportsmanship but most importantly respect for yourself. It is about your own "self worth".

Introduction

Coach Eoannou's "A Winner's Five Respects" is both a philosophy for boxing and a philosophy for life. We invite you to read and study BOXING: ESSENTIAL SKILLS. With determination and dedication you can learn the skills to perform the magnificent sport of amateur boxing at a championship level, which always begins with mastering the essentials.

We divided BOXING: ESSENTIAL SKILLS into 15 parts.

PART 1: THE BEGINNING

This part includes the background of Coach Eoannou, his philosophy summarized in "A Winner's Five Respects" along with tips and suggestions of how to find a place to train, which coaches and gyms to consider attending, and which coaches and gyms to avoid. In addition, you will learn all about essential equipment; tools of the trade needed for training, including how to wrap your own hands or someone else's hands; and the other equipment required, preparing you for the "Ring Drills" and the sparring sessions.

PART 2: DAILY PRACTICE SESSIONS at the GYM

This part includes the daily practice schedule used at the gym which is essential to entrench the skills (footwork and punching) and the conditioning required before you progress to the "Ring Drills" and sparring. These essential skills must be mastered before progressing to preparation for competition, which may someday allow you to compete for a championship.

PART 3: LESSONS FOR THE RIGHT-HANDED BOXER

In only 23 lessons, this part contains all the essential boxing skills for beginners, including all the essential footwork, the first 3 punches, the first 2 combinations and the first 3 angles, ONLY for the Right-Handed Boxer.

PART 4: DVD 1   VIDEO FOR THE NOVICE RIGHT-HANDED BOXER A. FUNDAMENTALS B. "RING DRILLS" AND SPARRING

This part covers the Fundamentals and "Ring Drills" including introduction to sparring for the beginner (novice) Right-Handed Boxer. The novice will learn to perform these "Ring Drills" against both a RIGHT-HANDED BOXER and a LEFT-HANDED BOXER on both OFFENSE and DEFENSE learning the following in detail:
1. How to throw the first 3 punches.
2. How to throw the first 2 combinations.
3. How to perform the essential footwork and develop the essential 3 angles.
4. How to defend against the first 3 punches.
5. How to throw counter punches against a RIGHT-HANDED opponent.
6. How to throw counter punches against a LEFT-HANDED opponent.
7. How to cut off the ring.
8. How to fight off the ropes.
9. How to fight out of a corner.

PART 5: LESSONS FOR THE LEFT-HANDED BOXER.

In only 23 lessons, this part contains all the essential boxing skills for beginners, including all the essential footwork, the first 3 punches, the first 2 combinations and the first 3 angles ONLY for the Left-Handed Boxer.

Introduction

PART 6: DVD 2 VIDEO FOR THE NOVICE LEFT-HANDED BOXER
A. FUNDAMENTALS
B. "RING DRILLS" AND SPARRING

This part covers the Fundamentals and "Ring Drills" including introduction to sparring for the beginner (novice) Left-Handed Boxer. The novice will learn to perform these "Ring Drills" against both a RIGHT-HANDED BOXER and a LEFT-HANDED BOXER on both OFFENSE and DEFENSE learning the following in detail:

1. How to throw the first 3 punches.
2. How to throw the first 2 combinations.
3. How to perform the essential footwork and develop the essential 3 angles.
4. How to defend against the first 3 punches.
5. How to throw counter punches against a RIGHT-HANDED opponent.
6. How to throw counter punches against a LEFT-HANDED opponent.
7. How to cut off the ring.
8. How to fight off the ropes.
9. How to fight out of a corner.

PART 7: ESSENTIAL RULES FOR "RING DRILLS" AND SPARRING

PART 8: 100 QUIZ QUESTIONS
A quiz of 100 questions based on all the essential material presented.
PART 9: GLOSSARY
Most of the essential language and definitions used in the amateur sport of boxing.
PART 10: ANSWERS TO 100 QUIZ QUESTIONS
Answers to the 100 quiz questions.
PART 11: REFERENCES FROM COACH DEAN EOANNOU
Books, videotapes and DVDs.
PART 12: THE APPENDIX
The 15 Must Have Boxing Books, Boxing Champions at the University at Buffalo Boxing Club, Boxing Equipment Web Sites, and Boxing Films (Movies).

PART 13: BOXING PERFORMANCE TESTS
COACH'S EVALUATION SHEETS

PART 14 : TABLE OF CONTENTS FOR DVD 1 VIDEO; DVD 2 VIDEO

PART 15: ACKNOWLEDGEMENTS

PART 16: CONCUSSION: HEAD INJURY

Part 1: The Beginning

1. The Buffalo System of Building Champions

What is the Buffalo System? This is the system created, designed and built by Coach Dean Eoannou, which underpins and supports the motto of the University at Buffalo Boxing Club, simply stated, "We Build Champions!" The Buffalo system is built on Coach Dean Eoannou's following concepts and principles:

a. **Newton's Second Law of Motion:** A forceful, powerful punch obeys Newton's Second Law of Motion which, for our purposes, states that F=MA, where F or force of the punch equals the M (mass) or the boxer's body weight, times A which stands for acceleration or speed of the punching motion. In other words, the power or force of the punch is increased if you transfer your body weight quickly. The faster you move your body weight the more powerful the force of your punch.

b. **Boxing off the Back Foot**: Boxing off the back foot refers to the boxer's ability to transfer the Mass (body weight) explosively to produce the forceful, powerful punch (F). This transferring of the boxer's body weight with each punch (not arm punching) results in power punching and occurs when moving the Mass (body weight) from back foot to the to the front foot or from the front foot to the back foot. The transfer of body weight is not always from one foot to another when throwing the jab the body weight (mass)movement is forward, but at the end of the punch the weight stays on the back foot as the arm returns to its initial starting position. The jab is discussed in detail during the lessons. It is this movement of your body weight (mass) that begins when you are learning to box off the back foot.

c. **Conditioning:** Conditioning for stamina and explosive movements with power punching is an essential for any champion boxer. Our detailed program is outlined in the book in PART **2: DAILY PRACTICE SESSIONS at the GYM** are essential to building our many amateur champions.

d. **Mastering Each Lesson – Step-by-Step:** The Buffalo System depends upon learning and MASTERING each skill (footwork and punches) before progressing to learning the next skill.

e. **"Ring Drills" and sparring:** After mastering the essential skills (footwork and punches) and passing the performance skills tests, the novice enters the ring to perform all the offensive and defensive drills against an experienced boxer without the fear of being hurt, the idea is to "teach not injure". Controlled sparring under the watchful eye of the coach ensures progressive skills development of the novice boxer.

f. **Preparation for the Next Level – Competition: Once the novice, learns, practices and passes all the essential skills tests (footwork and punches) along with the conditioning tests and has performed and passed the "Ring Drills" and sparring tests (all the necessary tests are listed and outlined in PART 12: APPENDIX pages 134-139) the boxer is ready, if desired, to prepare for competition.** It usually takes about 3 to 6 months of training at the novice level, which is everything taught in this book, BOXING: ESSENTIAL SKILLS, before you are ready to perform the "Ring Drills" and sparring and then, at the direction of the coach, you may move on to the next level, preparing for competition, which includes learning the next 6 punches and enhancing your overall physical and mental conditioning.

2. Who is Coach Dean Eoannou (E-O-WAN-NEW)

Born in Buffalo, New York in 1953, Coach Dean Eoannou graduated in 1976 with a Bachelor's Degree in Environmental Education from Cornell University in Ithaca, New York. After a 23 year career as a floor manager at the Ford Motor Stamping plant in Buffalo, he retired to follow his passion as the coach for the State University of New York at Buffalo (UB) Boxing Club in 2006.

Coach's early boxing mentors were Johnny Sudac Jr. and Sam Gibson at Buffalo's Singer's Gym founded by amateur boxer, manager and promoter Jack Singer in the 1920's. From 1969 to 1972, Johnny Sudac Jr. trained Coach Eoannou along with a number of notable "good fighters" including Ralph Racine, Hank Pelow and Al Quinney. Top ranked light heavy weight Jimmy Ralston also trained at Singer's Gym during Johnny Sudac Jr.'s era. With over 30 years of experience as a trainer and coach, Dean Eoannou became the UB Boxing Club Coach in 2004. Taking students, most without prior athletic or boxing experience, Coach Eoannou teaches boxing and produces champions. In the first 7 years directing the UB Boxing Club team, Coach Eoannou trained 16 champions, (4 women and 12 men) earning 24 New York State Golden Gloves Championships, 3 New York State Empire Games State Champions and 1 Northeast Champion for a total of 28 Championships in all. In addition, Coach Eoannou has trained a National Golden Gloves Bronze Medalist and a US National Silver Medalist. A significant honor, "Amateur Boxer of the Year" (2008) was awarded to Wendy Casey by the Buffalo Veteran Boxers Association Ring 44. Miss Casey is the first woman ever to achieve this acclaim from the venerable organization, and she is one of the four women Golden Gloves Champions Coach Eoannou has trained.

Recently, Coach Eoannou received the Champions Award from his numerous (16) University of Buffalo Boxing Club champions as a token of their appreciation and respect for his teaching excellence and supreme dedication to the amateur sport of boxing and most importantly for his great concern regarding the welfare of his women and men athletes. Coach still resides in Buffalo with his wife Kelly of over 30 years and their two daughters Kylie and Casey.

3. Coach Dean Eoannou's Philosophy Statement: Coach as a Responsible Teacher

The coach's essential role is that of a teacher of boxing skills with the goal of fully developing the boxer's talents and potential. The coach's first responsibility is the boxer's health and well-being.

Fundamental to success is the teaching of essential skills piece by piece, like building blocks from balance, Stance or Boxing Position (Set Position), footwork, punches, shadow boxing, range, rhythm drills, conditioning, "Ring Drills", sparring and ultimately, if desired, competition. Each of the building blocks must be taught by the Coach, successfully learned, accomplished, perfectly reproduced, and mastered by the student before the next building block is approached; otherwise, the result is a flawed boxer. Boxing is learned. There are no naturals. Mastering each skill is mandatory before proceeding to the next skill. Each succeeding skill functions as an essential building block growing and building the boxer from the "ground" up.

With realistic goals, the young boxer develops all the requisite skills necessary to succeed while growing self-confidence and reaching the goals set by both the coach and athlete. Coach develops an individualized style based on the natural physical attributes of each athlete. During the "Ring Drills" and sparring sessions, Coach is ALWAYS present and uses these opportunities as lessons in growth and development with the idea that "Rings Drills" and sparring are teaching sessions not "fighting" sessions; the idea is to "teach not injure".

Coach's commitment to the athlete's best interest, builds the essential ingredients of trust and respect. The coach/athlete relationship demands these qualities of respect and trust, especially during competition with the boxer, trusting the direction given between rounds by the coach is vital during the "heat of battle".

As a responsible teacher, Coach Eoannou's preaches a philosophy of respect.

Part 1: The Beginning

Coach lists a WINNER'S FIVE RESPECTS:

1. RESPECT YOURSELF: You accomplish this by keeping a drug-free body, eating a healthy diet and getting the conditioning and rest you need.

2. RESPECT EVERYONE ELSE: You accomplish this by treating coaches, teammates, opponents and officials with respect. It's a reflection of your own personal dignity and character.

3. RESPECT PRACTICE: You accomplish this by working hard, competing and getting better each and every day.

4. RESPECT FINISHING: You accomplish this by finishing every drill, every practice and every competition with full effort. There is no excuse for laziness!

5. RESPECT THE SPORT AND SPORTSMANSHIP: You accomplish this by behaving like a champion inside and outside of the ring.

Adversity reveals your character by "how you fight the fight". Boxing can teach life lessons in courage, discipline, hard work, determination (heart), integrity and self worth that truly eclipse any win/loss record.

4. Finding a place to train

a. The Coach

It is all about the coach. Find a coach who is truly interested and experienced in teaching boxing skills to the beginner (novice). It is the coach's responsibility to develop the new boxer. Find someone who cares about the well-being of each boxing student. Go on-line, obtain the name of local gyms and boxing clubs, and then visit and observe. Look at the walls in the gym. Is there a history with posters and champions produced at that gym by that coach? If a coach has limited experience developing young boxers or if few boxers have competed in boxing tournaments, avoid that gym.

Go to several local boxing tournaments and determine which local clubs and coaches "stand out". Ask questions of the other boxers about their coaches. For example, ask the open question to a prospective coach, "As a beginning boxing student what can I expect?" Ask directly how much time the coach will spend developing you. Ask about how much time is required preparing you for your first serious sparring and for your first competitive boxing match. If, on the other hand, exercise is your main interest in learning boxing, make that objective clearly known to your prospective coach.

Carefully observe how your prospective coach handles sparring sessions. Are there two inexperienced boxers hurting each other or is the coach controlling the sparring sessions by always being ringside and assuring that no one is deliberately injured? How does the coach determine readiness for serious sparring? A responsible coach is ALWAYS on the ring apron, stopping the sparring session, speaking, teaching, correcting and focusing on improving the skills of each boxer. It is best to be at a gym where the coach gives you specific directions for developing and improving your skills so you can enter the ring for the "Ring Drills" with a more experienced boxer who will not hurt you. The goal is teaching, learning and development, not humiliating, beating and discouragement.

Ask how the coach determines the optimal weight class in which you should be competing. Find out if your coach has a relationship with other coaches at other gyms and institutions so matches are arranged honestly and fairly so you are not advanced rapidly and prematurely matched against more skillful and experienced boxers. Keep searching until you find the right person to coach you.

b. The Gym

Look at the equipment available at the gym and ask if this gym has the most "up-to-date" modern equipment. Ask who will oversee your sport-specific exercise and conditioning program. Ask which equipment and what exercises will teach you to become a better boxer. The gym must have the equipment and the coaching staff that understands strength and conditioning exercises, including weight training and plyometrics, which are fundamental to modern training in amateur boxing. Boxing and conditioning have changed. Athletes are stronger and the gym must have modern equipment with an experienced coaching staff that can enable you to train safely.

c. Female Boxers

As a female, it is important to determine if the coach has experience training other females since all athletes, females and males, need to feel safe in a mature, professional, harassment-free training environment. Established women boxers are proud of their competitive achievements having crossed a line few women have crossed. Boxing changes women physically with strength, endurance, and long lean muscles, mentally with confidence and assurance that they can legitimately defend themselves against almost any man who is not a trained boxer. That is empowering. As a beginning female boxer new to a particular gym, remember to respect the established male and female boxers by arriving at the boxing gym practice sessions as an athlete dressed appropriately. Modesty is always prudent. Be yourself and avoid confrontation by being respectful; otherwise, the seasoned female sparring partners may resent you and will likely compete against you more intensively than normal. You are an amateur athlete in training. Respecting yourself and all the other athletes at your gym is wise.

d. What to look for

1. **Coaches and Gyms to consider when:**
    a. There is a willingness to teach beginners.
    b. There is experience in developing young boxers.
    c. There is an atmosphere of learning and camaraderie.
    d. There is sufficient equipment.
    e. There is a history of competition and a winning tradition.
    f. The coach matches sparring sessions for novices with experienced boxers who are also willing to teach and not injure the younger boxers.
    g. The coach is ALWAYS present during "Ring Drills" and sparring sessions with commitment to safety.
    h. The coach develops each boxer's style differently based on the individual's ability and natural physical attributes.
    i. The coach protects the club's boxers during competition by insuring the boxers are evenly matched.
    j. The coach possesses leadership qualities and directs the program professionally, building champions.

2. **Coaches and Gyms to avoid when:**
    a. There is an unwillingness to teach beginners.

Part 1: The Beginning

    b. There is limited or no experience in developing young boxers.

    c. There is an atmosphere of indifference to learning and limited camaraderie.

    d. There is insufficient equipment.

    e. There is limited or no history of competition.

    f. The coach mismatches sparring sessions as these sessions become "fights" with limited learning.

    g. The coach frequently is ABSENT during sparring sessions.

    h. The coach develops all of the boxers similarly with a philosophy of the "optimal style"; "cookie cutting" the boxers.

    i. The coach is nonchalant about over matching the club's boxers during competition. Should over matching occur, it's considered a "learning" experience.

    j. The coach lacks leadership ability, allowing the parents and boxers to direct the program.

3. Questions to ask your prospective coach:

    a. How many beginning or novice boxers (male and female) have you trained in the past few years?

    b. How many beginning or novice boxers (male and female) are you training now?

    c. As a beginning boxer, what can I expect?

    d. How much time do you devote to a beginning boxer?

    e. What "benchmark" skills do you use to determine readiness for serious sparring?

    f. What "benchmark" skills do you use to determine readiness for competition at the sub novice level?

    g. How do you determine and develop a boxer's style?

    h. How do you determine the weight class in which I should compete?

    i. How do you determine whom I should eventually be matched against in competition?

    j. Who will oversee and teach the proper exercise and conditioning programs for a beginning boxer?

    k. How many champions (male and female) have you personally produced?

5. Getting Started

a. Personal equipment: Tools of the trade for training

1) Jump ropes

    a) What to buy

(1) The vinyl (plastic) rope: There are a number of ropes on the market that you can buy; however, a good place to start is the most inexpensive, fast turning, vinyl (plastic) rope since you can adjust it to your height merely by putting a knot under the grip handles.

(2) The beaded jump rope: This is also a good first choice since it is durable requiring minimal care. It comes in 3 sizes (7 foot, 8 foot and 9 foot lengths), which can also be adjusted for your height by placing a knot in the rope near the grip handles.

(3) The cable rope: This is a more expensive rope that is cut to your height and is the fastest turning rope on the market since it contains ball-bearings in the handles, allowing for the generation of great speed.

(4) The leather rope: This is also called the classic speed rope, and it is popular but not as fast as the vinyl, beaded or cable ropes. It is also adjustable to your height by tying a knot under the grip handles.

(5) **The white rope or clothes line rope**: This is not recommended since it is too slow for the rhythm required for boxing.

b) How to measure

To measure or "size a rope", it is best to stand on the rope with both feet a shoulder's width apart. The grip handles of the rope should be level with your waist. If the rope does not come up to the level of your waist, it is too short. Get a longer rope and re-measure it. If the rope is too long, tie a knot or two knots under the grip handles and re-measure. After finding a rope of the correct length (which should come up to the level of your waist), you can start learning to jump rope like a boxer.

c) How to use

Jumping rope is essential for learning coordination, rhythm and timing, and it is the first step to overall aerobic conditioning. Jumping rope is the first thing you do in the gym after wrapping your hands. Start out slowly and be sure to jump on the balls of the feet and **DO NOT** jump flatfooted.

(1) **Two feet**: This is the simplest way to start out jumping rope—one revolution of the rope to one jump with both of your feet. You can start jumping for 30 seconds and resting for 1 minute. Work your way up to jumping for 3 minutes (1 round), rest for 1 minute and repeat jumping for another 3 minutes until you are able to jump rope for three 3-minute rounds as your warm-up in preparation for your daily practice sessions.

(2) **Alternate feet**: Once you are able to jump rope for 3 three-minute rounds with a 1 minute rest between rounds, you can alter your routine. For example, the "alternate feet" routine includes 4 jumps with both feet, then 4 jumps on the right foot only followed by 4 jumps on the left foot only. The next progression in the routine includes 3 jumps with both feet, then 3 jumps on the right foot only followed by 3 jumps on the left foot only. The next progression in the routine includes 2 jumps with both feet, then 2 jumps on the right foot only followed by 2 jumps on the left foot only. Next, 1 jump with both feet then 1 jump on the right foot only followed by 1 jump on the left foot only. Then back to 4 jumps with both feet and so forth. You repeat this routine of 4, 3, 2 and 1 for the full 3 minutes and for 3 rounds with a 1 minute rest between rounds.

(3) **Crisscross**: Learning the crisscross is learning the "boxer's dance," which takes some time to learn. Probably the best way to learn the crisscross is to watch another boxer performing the crisscross and then trying it on your own. Be sure that you cross your hands about waist height in front of you as you jump over the crossed rope. This takes effort to learn, so be persistent and continue trying on a daily basis and you will learn to do the crisscross and after learning the crisscross you are on your way to becoming a boxer.

2) Hand wraps

a) What to buy

The 180-inch wraps: The 180-inch "Mexican wraps" are the best wraps to buy since these wraps are long enough for an adult sized hand and are made from fabric that does NOT stretch. These inelastic "Mexican wraps" helps in preventing injury to your hands while training. There are many other types of wraps on the market, some containing stretch fabrics that do not provide the essential protection for your hands and are best avoided. Use only **inelastic 180-inch non-stretch fabric** when wrapping your hands.

Part 1: The Beginning

The procedure, technical steps, used for wrapping your hands is the same for training, "Ring Drills" and sparring. Gauze wraps and tape rather than the "Mexican wraps" are the inelastic materials exclusively used for competition.

b) Care and washing of the wraps

You should buy 2 sets of 180-inch inelastic hand wraps so one can be washed and dried while you are using the other one. Mesh hand wrap wash bags are useful for preventing tangling when machine washing your wraps. Often the gym will have a metal Hand Wrap Roller so you can rewind your hand wraps back into a roll for easy reapplication to your hands after washing. Visit one of the equipment web sites found in **PART 12: APPENDIX** or a sporting goods store for these pieces of equipment.

c) How to wrap your own hands and another boxer's hands

You need to perfect the wrapping of your own hands, since these wraps are used in your daily practice sessions at the gym. Study both the photographs and DVD, which "walks" you through the entire process of wrapping your own hands systematically. The photos and DVD will also teach you to wrap a teammate's hands when and if you are called upon to teach another novice boxer this essential skill.

(1) Wrapping your own hands (photographs 1-1 to 1-44) VIDEO CLIPS

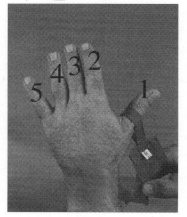

1-1 Hand wraps. A. Scissors B. Gauze C. 1-inch cloth tape D. Hand wraps-One for each hand

1-2 HOW TO WRAP YOUR OWN LEFT HAND. Spread your fingers apart as wide as possible. Applying the (RED) wrap onto the thumb. Finger #1--Thumb, Finger #2--Index finger, Finger #3--Middle finger, Finger #4--Ring finger, Finger #5-Pinky finger.

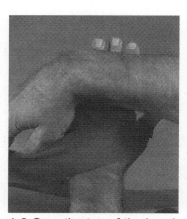

1-3 Over the top of the hand.

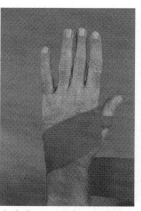

1-4 Around the wrist 4.

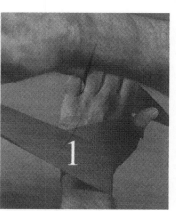

1-5 Over the wrist #1.

1-6 Tighten under the wrist.

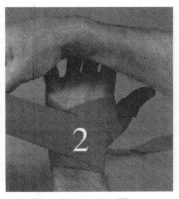

1-7 Over the wrist #2.

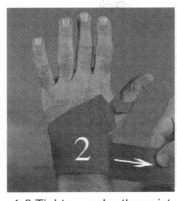

1-8 Tighten under the wrist. (arrow)

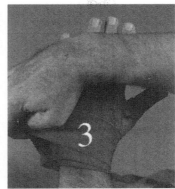

1-9 Over the wrist #3.

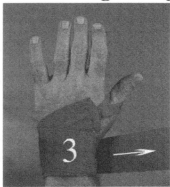

1-10 Tighten under the wrist. (arrow)

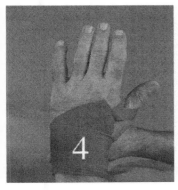

1-11 Over the wrist #4.

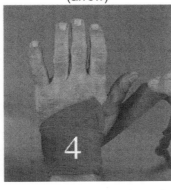

1-12 Tighten under the wrist approaching the thumb.

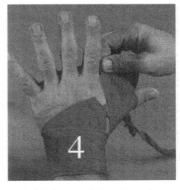

1-13 Around the thumb.

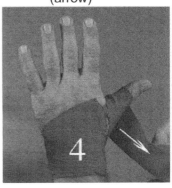

1-14 Tighten under the thumb (arrow)

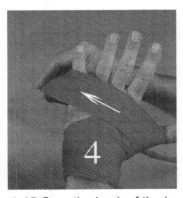

1-15 Over the back of the hand. (arrow—direction of pull)

1-16 Tighten under the hand. (arrow)

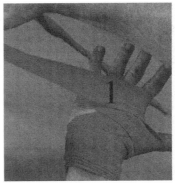

1-17 Around the knuckles #1.

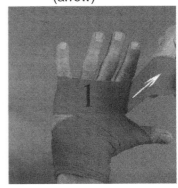

1-18 Tighten under the hand. (arrow)

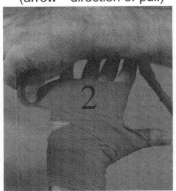

1-19 Around the knuckles #2.

1-20 Tighten under the hand. (arrow)

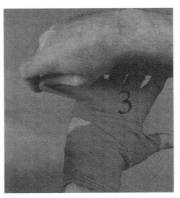

1-21 Around the knuckles #3.

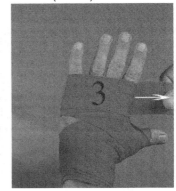

1-22 Tighten under the hand. (arrow)

23

Part 1: The Beginning

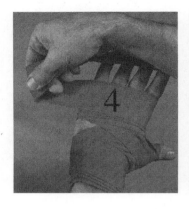

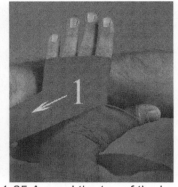

1-23 Around the knuckles #4.

1-24 Tighten under the hand. (arrow)

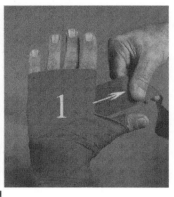

1-25 Around the top of the hand angled toward the wrist (arrow #1).

1-26 Tighten under the hand. (arrow)

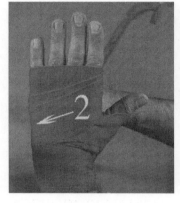

1-27 Around the top of the hand angled towards the wrist. (arrow) #2

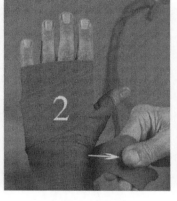

1-28 Tighten up the wrist at the base of the thumb. (arrow)

1-29 Advance between finger #2 (index finger) and finger #3 (middle finger) (arrow #1)

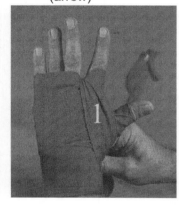

1-30 Tighten under the hand at the base of the thumb.

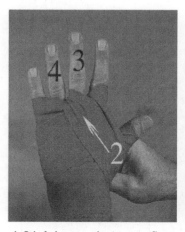

1-31 Advance between finger #3 (middle finger) and finger #4 (ring finger) (arrow #2)

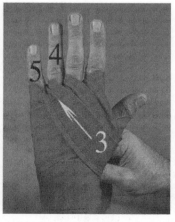

1-32 Advance between finger #4 (ring finger) and finger # 5 (pinky finger) (arrow #3)

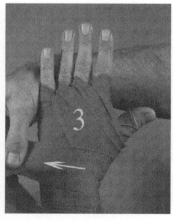

1-33 Tighten under the hand and advance over the wrist. (arrow)

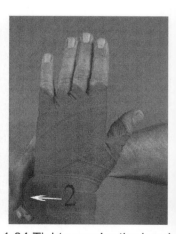

1-34 Tighten under the hand. (arrow)

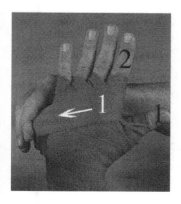

1-35 Advance between finger #1 (the thumb) and finger #2 (index finger) around the top of the hand angled toward the wrist.

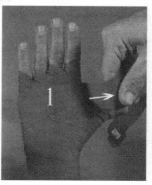

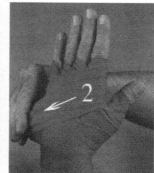

1-37 Advance between finger #1 (the thumb) and finger #2 (index finger) around the top of the hand angled toward the wrist a second time.

1-36 Tighten under the hand.

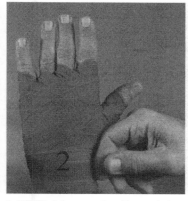

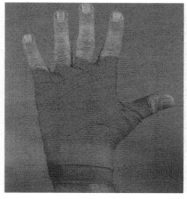

1-38 Tighten under the wrist, secure with Velcro.

1-39 Wrapping complete.

1-40 Ready for action.

Wrapping another boxer's hands (photographs 1-45 to 1-85) **VIDEO CLIPS**

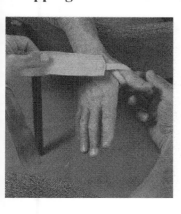

1-41 HOW TO WRAP ANOTHER BOXER'S RIGHT HAND. Have the boxer spread his/her fingers as wide as possible. Applying the (YELLOW) wrap on to the thumb and over the top of the wrist. (arrow) Finger # 1 (the thumb), Finger # 2 (the index finger), Finger # 3 (the middle finger) Finger # 4 (the ring finger), Finger # 5 (the finger pinky).

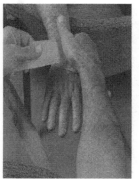

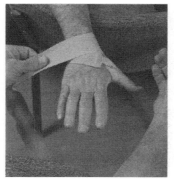

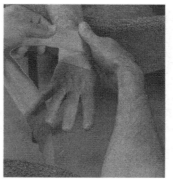

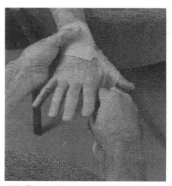

1-42 Over the wrist #2.

1-43 Over the wrist #3.

1-44 Over the wrist #4.

1-45 Over the top of the thumb.

Part 1: The Beginning

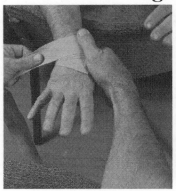

1-46 Wrap around the thumb.

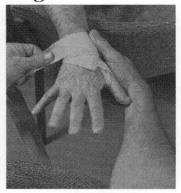

1-47 Over the top of the hand.

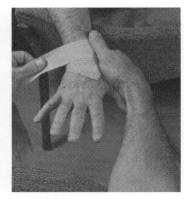

1-48 Tighten under the hand.

1-49 Around the thumb.

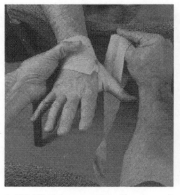

1-50 Tighten under the hand

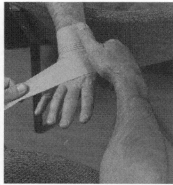

1-51 Aound the knuckles #2.

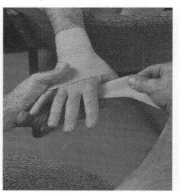

1-52 Tighten under the hand.

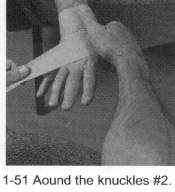

1-53-Around the knuckles #3.

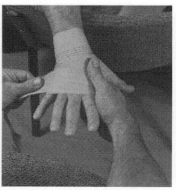

1-54 Tighten under the hand.

1-55 Around the knuckles #4.

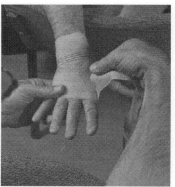

1-56 Tighten under the hand.

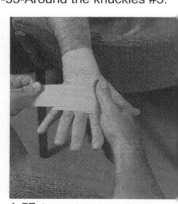

1-57 Around the top of the hand angled toward the wrist.

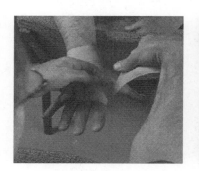

1-58 Tighten under the hand.

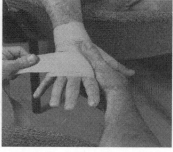

1-59 Around the top of the hand angled toward the wrist.

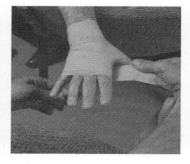

1-60 Tighten under the wrist near the base of the thumb.

1-61 Advance between finger #2 (index finger) and the finger #3 (middle finger)

1-62 Tighten under the hand wrist near the base of the thumb.

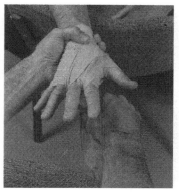

1-63 Advanced between finger # 3 (middle finger) and finger #4 (ring finger)

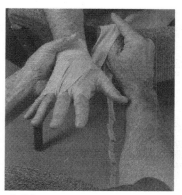

1-64 Tighten under the wrist near the base of the thumb.

1-65 Advance between finger #4 (ring finger) and finger #5 (pinky finger)

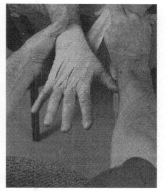

1-66 Tighten under the wrist.

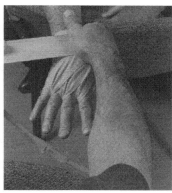

1-67 Advance over the wrist.

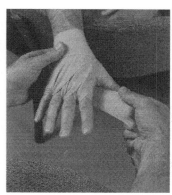

1-68 Tighten under the hand.

1-69 Advance between finger #1 (the thumb) and finger #2 (index finger) around the top of the hand angled towards the wrist)

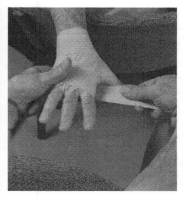

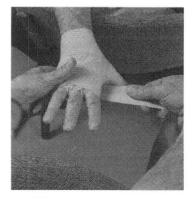

1-70 Tighten under the hand.

1-71 Advance between finger #1 (the thumb) and finger # 2 (index finger) around the top of the hand angled toward the wrist a second time.

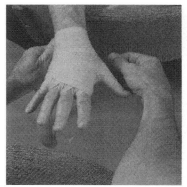

1-72 Tighten under the hand.

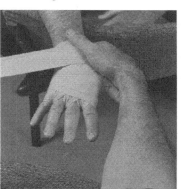

1-73 Tighten under the hand.

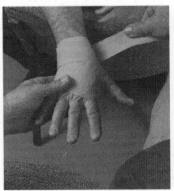
1-74 Tighten under the wrist.

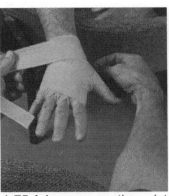
1-75 Advance over the wrist again.

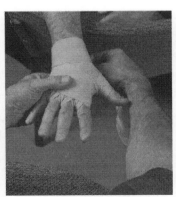
1-76 Tighten under the wrist.

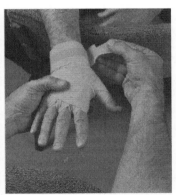
1-77 Secure with Velcro.

1-78 Wrapping complete.

1-79 Ready for action.

3) Boxing Gloves

a) Types and weights

There are many different types of boxing gloves used for training on the speed bag and heavy bag as well as different weights of gloves, ranging from 6 ounces 8, 10, 12, 14, 16, 18 to 20 ounces; and there are various methods of tightening and securing the gloves to your wrists. The gloves we recommend for beginners (the novice) are 16-ounce gloves for training (daily practice sessions) and for "Ring Drills" and sparring. For your information, there are also Youth Gloves and Women's Boxing Gloves. For other types of gloves, visit one of the equipment web sites found in **PART 12: APPENDIX** or a sporting goods store for these pieces of equipment.

(1) Velcro wristband 16-ounce gloves used for training (daily practice sessions): Velcro wristband 16-ounce gloves are practical, since placing them on and taking them off is easy. The **advantage** of the Velcro gloves is that you can quickly put the gloves on yourself without help from the coach or a teammate. We prefer the heavy 16-ounce gloves for training, since lighter gloves (10-ounce or 12-ounce) used in competition will feel much lighter than the 16-ounce training gloves. In addition, by using the 16-ounce gloves, we are cutting down the risk of injury to either boxer's hands or any body part of the sparring partner, especially the sparring partner's face. Occasionally, we suggest Gel gloves or 20-ounce gloves to give additional protection to a boxer's hands. (1-86a)

(2) Lace-up wristband 16-ounce gloves used for sparring: Gloves with a lace-up wristband are used for sparring. We use the 16-ounce variety, which requires the coach or a teammate to tighten the laces, securing the gloves to your wrist. The lace-up gloves are advantageous since they lessen the chance of injuring your sparring partner since the laces are taped while the Velcro gloves can scrape or abrade your sparring partner's skin or eyes. (1-86b)

(a) Velcro wristband 16-ounce gloves: For training and "Ring Drills" (1-80a)

(b) Lace-up wristband 16-ounce gloves: For "Ring Drills" and sparring (1-80b)

1-80 Shoes a) high b) med c) low

4) Shoes for training (workout)

In general, your shoes for training, "Ring Drills" or sparring must be smooth, flat-bottom shoes ("worn soles") that allow for smooth footwork, facilitating your ability to slide on either the gym floor or on the canvas floor in the ring. Whether you choose low or high top shoes is purely your own individual preference. Choose comfortable smooth-sole shoes (**not running shoes**) and a pair of athletic socks for your daily training practice sessions at the gym. Practice shoes: (1-81)

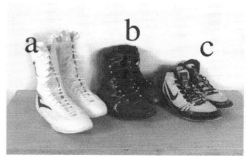

a) High   b) Medium height   c) Low

1-81 Shoes a) high b) med c) low

5) Trunks (contrasting waistband)

a) Practice: Use any comfortable trunks (shorts) or sweatpants as long as you can easily move without restricting your movements.

b) Competition: Requires that the boxer wear specific trunks with a contrasting waistband so the judges can easily determine if a boxer received a blow (punch) below the contrasting waistband. A blow (punch) below the contrasting waistband is called a "low blow" and is a foul. The offending boxer will be warned by the referee and will lose points. (1-81)

1-81 Competition trunks

6) Shirt

a) Practice: Any comfortable shirt of your choice is fine.

b) Competition: Requires a sleeveless shirt.

b. Equipment for Skills Training and Conditioning

This section presents an introduction to the essential tools for skills training and conditioning.
PART 2: DAILY GYM PRACTICE SESSIONS including how to use the equipment.

Part 1: The Beginning

1) **Heavy bag:** Is useful in learning many aspects of boxing essentials:1) footwork skills and developing angles, 2) understanding the concept of range and how to box within the optimum range for effective punching and reaching the MMF (the Moment of Maximum Force) of your punches, 3) refining your punching skills and further understanding the MMF, and 4) further enhancing your anaerobic conditioning. (1-82)

1-82 Heavy Bag

1-83 Double ended bag

2) **Double ended bag**: Promotes hand-eye coordination and timing since it is a faster moving bag than the Heavy Bag. (1-90)

3) **Upper cut bag:** This bag rapidly changes rhythm and direction, requiring footwork, timing and range adjustments by the boxer to the bag's unpredictable movements. (1-84)

1-84 Upper cut bag

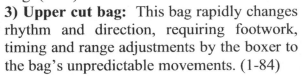

1-85 Speed bag

4) **Speed bag**: Using this bag promotes the development of your hand-eye coordination and your ability to time the movements of the bag so you can strike the bag at the exact moment, learning effective and efficient punching skills. (1-85)

5) **Mitts -Also called Punch Mitts or Focus Pads or Strike Pads:** By using the mitts, the coach can directly assess the student's punching techniques, thereby allowing the coach to teach and correct the student's flaws.

The coach can call for different punch combinations on offense and defense and assess the student with the same view as an opponent would have. With the coach using the mitts, it is an excellent way for coach to access the boxer's anaerobic conditioning since the coach dictates the pace and duration of these punching drills. The coach's use of the mitts is also excellent for the student since this exercise requires further development of hand-eye coordination, sharpens punching skills, footwork, further understanding of range, and enhances anaerobic conditioning. Use of the mitts by the coach is an essential part of the student's learning process. (1-86)

1-86 Mitts

6) Weights: Weights are used to develop and improve strength, but the weights are also used to develop the explosive acceleration (mobilizing the fast twitch muscles) needed to produce forceful punches. All of the weight exercises are performed at 50% of the maximum weight the boxer is able to move during one repetition. This is "50% of the one rep max". For example, if the boxer is able to perform only one repetition of a shoulder press with 100 pounds of weight then the shoulder press exercises will be performed at 50 pounds of weight. Therefore, 50 pounds is 50% of 100 pounds and "50% of the one rep max".

a) Straight bar weights: The straight bar is used primarily for shoulder press exercises at 50 % of the "one rep max". The straight bar weights used in our gym range from 10 pounds to 50 pounds. (1-87)

1-87 Straight bar weights

b) Dumbbell weights: All the weight exercises performed with dumbbells are also performed at 50% of the "one rep max" with the exception of some punching exercises where the 3-pound dumbbell weights are used since the training gloves are 16 ounces (one pound). Dumbbell weights that are used in the University's gym range from 3 pounds to 50 pounds. (1-88)

1-88 Dumbbell weights

7) Plyometric boxes: All of the plyometric exercises are performed to develop the fast twitch muscles and explosive acceleration of the arms and legs. These exercises are performed with the end-point of "loss of explosiveness". All of these plyometric exercises are described in detail in **PART 2: DAILY PRACTICE SESSIONS at the GYM**

1-89 a & b plyometric boxes

a) **12-inch and 6-inch high boxes: (1-89a, b)**
   Plyometric boxes:
   (1) 12-inch high box (for vertical jumps)
   (2) 6-inch high box (for push-ups)
   (3) Two 6-inch high boxes (for push-ups) (1-90c)

b) **Lateral movement boxes:**
   Plyometric boxes for lateral movement exercises (for lateral jumps). (1-91)

1-90 c Plyometric boxes

1-91 c Lateral movement boxes

8) Core machines: Strong abdominal muscles (core muscles) are essential for throwing a punch and for receiving ("taking") a punch and protecting the underlying organs in the stomach (abdomen) such as the liver.

PART 2: DAILY PRACTICE SESSIONS at the GYM covers how to use the equipment and the routines essential to developing a strong core.

Part 1: The Beginning

a) **Roman chair:** Roman Chair is a machine useful in developing a strong core. (1-98)

b) **Sit-up bench:** Incline/decline sit-up bench is a machine useful in developing a strong core. (1-93)

9) **Medicine balls:** Medicine balls are used for sit-ups and rolls that vary in weight from 6 pounds to 15 pounds. (1-94)

1-92 Roman Chair

1-93 Sit-up bench

1-94 Medicine balls

1-95 Timing bell (interval timer)

Timing bell (interval timer): The timing bell is an essential piece of equipment for every gym. The duration or time of a round can be altered and set for 2 or 3 minutes a round with the rest periods between rounds adjusted to either 30 seconds or 1 minute. A loud bell is usually part of the timer, denoting when a round starts and stops. In addition, some timers have a large digital display showing the time left in a round. Other timers use a lighting system where the red light signifies the rest period, the green light is on for the duration of the round and yellow light is on for the last 30 seconds remaining of the round. Personal timers and training timers are also available for the student and can be purchased from one of the equipment web sites found in the PART 12: APPENDIX or a sporting goods store. These pieces of personal equipment (personal or training timers are optional since every boxing gym has a timing bell. (1-95) Close-up of timing bell control panel. (1-96)

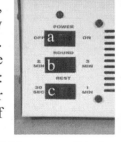

1-96 Close-up of timing bell control panel (a,b,c)

    a) **Power (on, off)**
    b) **Round duration options: 2 minutes or 3 minutes**
    c) **Rest duration options: 30 seconds or 60 seconds (1 minute)**

6. **Equipment for "Ring Drills" and sparring**

a. **Ring:** The ring has specific requirements. The minimum size for an amateur ring is 16-feet square, and the maximum size is 20-feet square. Professionals usually fight in a ring that is 18feet square, though the maximum allowable size is 22-feet square. The corners have padded posts that stand 58 inches high. Connecting the posts and enclosing the ring are four horizontal ropes per side. The floor of the ring is padded and covered with canvas and must extend at least two feet beyond the ropes (this part of the ring extending beyond the ropes is called the ring apron.) The height of the ring floor must be less than 4 feet above the ground for competition.

b. **Mouthpiece**—Mouth guards: There are various types of mouth guards used to protect the teeth in the upper and lower jaw. They must fit comfortably. Some newer designs use modern gel technology for mouth guards and some are designed with air channels, which allow the boxer to breathe while the mouth guard is in place. Some of the standard mouth guards do not have a breathing channel and come as a single guard (for upper or lower teeth only). We advise a double guard, protecting both the upper and lower teeth with a breathing channel for both breathing and speaking. If you have dental problems or wear braces, it best to see your dentist for advice and a fitting for a custom molded mouth guard. You can visit one of the equipment web sites found in **PART 12: APPENDIX** or a sporting goods store for these pieces of equipment. (1-1-97a)

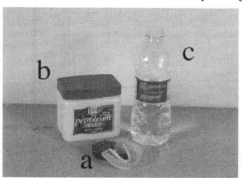

1-97 Mouthpieces: a) Mouth guards b) Petroleum jelly c) water bottle

1) How do you care for your mouth guard? Many mouth guards are plastic and can be boiled and cleaned. It is best to have a mouth guard case to protect your mouth guard from germs (bacteria, fungi and viruses). Be sure to **RINSE (WASH)** your mouth guard each time after using it. You should also wash it with an antibacterial agent (like Listerine or Scope) to keep your mouth guard clean and fresh.

b. Vaseline (Petroleum Jelly) is used, especially when sparring, to protect your face.

c. Water Bottle: It is essential that you bring a plastic water bottle to your daily practice session and maintain your hydration at all times. The type and style is your individual preference, but it must be made of some type of plastic since we do not want broken glass in the gym. (1-97c)

d. Contact lenses: If you need glasses, try soft contact lenses since they are safe to use and acceptable to USA Boxing, the controlling organization for Amateur Boxing.

f. Headgear:

1) **Types**: There are many different types of leather headgear. We advise headgear with a padded, molded plastic face bar to protect your face and nose from punches. Some boxers feel that the face bar limits their visibility so they prefer headgear without the face bar. Even if you do not want the face bar, be sure to buy headgear that will protect your forehead, cheeks and ears.
   a. Headgear without a nose bar. (1-104a)
   b. Headgear with a nose bar. (1-104b)

1-98a Headgear without nose bar-note black arrow top laces, red arrow back laces

2) **Proper Fit**: It is essential to properly fit your headgear with the two sets of adjustable laces found on each headgear. One set of adjustable laces is at the back of the headgear. (1-104a-red arrow) The other set of adjustable laces is at the top of the headgear. (1-104a-black arrow) (1-104b-black arrows). The adjustable laces that tie at the back of the headgear will secure the headgear to your head, preventing the headgear from slipping down and

1-99 Headgear with nose bar-note black arrow top laces

Part 1: The Beginning

keeping it tight. The adjustable laces that tie at the top of the headgear will keep it from falling down over your forehead and covering your eyes. You must protect your forehead, so secure your headgear just immediately above your eyebrows (on the bone just over your eye socket.)

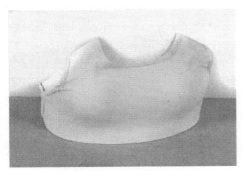

1-105 Chest protectors

g. Chest protector (Female): Many of our female boxers use the chest protector, and we recommend that you try this for protection and comfort. The chest protector (female) is recommended. (1-105)

h. Groin protector (Male): Essential for the male boxer is the protective cup. Some have elastic leg straps while others do not. Use the cup that feels most comfortable to you. The groin protector (male) is essential. (1-106)

1-106 Groin protectors (Male)

i. **Spit" bucket**: This is essential during "Ring Drills" and sparring sessions as we rinse the mouth guard over the bucket. We do not want water on the floor of the ring since a boxer might slip, fall and hurt him/herself.

j. **Tape: 1"athletic cloth tape**

PART 2: DAILY PRACTICE SESSIONS at the GYM

1. Introduction

This part includes the schedule for the daily practice sessions at the gym **(Monday to Saturday).** It is best to **plan for 2 hours each day, 6 days a week for each practice session.** This is the time needed to entrench the skills (footwork and punches) and the conditioning required before you can progress to the "Ring Drills" and sparring. These essential skills (footwork and punches), conditioning, "Ring Drills" and sparring must be **MASTERED** before progressing to preparation for competition, which may someday allow you to compete for a championship. An unofficial subtitle of this book, <u>BOXING: ESSENTIAL SKILLS,</u> could easily read "the art, science and practice" of boxing because skillful boxing is artful where the term art, refers to the mastery of a given skill. We truly believe that mastering the skill of boxing is an art form. Understanding the science of physics and its application to power punching using Newton's second law of motion, enables the boxer to realize the importance of speed, boxing off the back foot with dynamic weight transfer and how the scientific application of plyometrics can influence and enhance your punching power.

Plyometrics is any exercise in which muscles are repeatedly and **rapidly** stretched ("loaded") and then contracted as in jumping high off the ground or pushing rapidly like repeated push-ups performed rapidly. Plyometric exercises are designed to develop explosive movements (with speed), which develops muscular power. Essential athletic fitness or "conditioning" is composed of four parts:

1. Strength (moving a given amount of weight.)
2. Speed (power is how fast you can move that given weight.)
3. Stamina or endurance of your body's response to stress and/or pain.
4. Flexibility of muscles, tendons and joints.

Part 2: Daily Practice Sessions at the Gym

Boxing is a physically demanding sport performed under **anaerobic** (without oxygen) conditions so training requires a scientific approach to maximize development of explosive power and stamina during training and in the ring during competition. The modern scientific approach includes weight training, plyometrics, core training and cardio-respiratory conditioning (cardio=heart and respiratory=lungs and breathing), emphasizing anaerobic (without oxygen) conditioning. By fast paced training, both the heart rate and breathing rate are increased significantly, simulating ring competition conditions. The conditioning and the skills (footwork and punches) training are both essential to develop offensive and defensive capability. Specifically, the science of plyometrics focuses on maximizing speed to produce increased explosive power by emphasizing quality not quantity of pushing exercises for the shoulders and arms and jumping exercises for the legs. Three sets of these plyometric exercises are performed until the boxer "loses explosiveness" with a 1 minute rest between sets. We know that effective training must be fast-paced, emphasizing both speed and power.

Our approach is 3 minutes of intense exercise (this deliberately exceeds normal amateur 2-minute rounds during competition) with a 30 to 60 second rest period (interval) between rounds. (Normally in amateur boxing the rest between rounds is 1 minute.) Our practice sessions at the gym concentrate on skills (footwork and punches) and conditioning with strength and power (where the two components of power are strength and speed) using plyometrics and agility, balance, flexibility, muscle endurance, and cardio-respiratory endurance with intense and challenging exercises and drills. For our training at the University each round is 3 minutes in duration with a 1 minute rest between rounds although at times only a 30 second rest period is used to challenge the athlete and improve conditioning.

. Skills Training- Schedule

The daily skills training at the gym are 6 days a week (**M,T,W,Th,F,S**) with Sundays off and are performed in the following order and sequence:

. Skills Training Sequencing at the Gym-The order you do things

After entering the gym and dressing, the **FIRST** thing you do is wrap your hands for practice. a. Wrap your hands.
  b. Jump Rope - 3 Rounds (as a beginner start out jumping for 30 to 60 seconds or longer if you can with a 1 minute rest between exercises and eventually work up to 3 minutes of jumping for 3 rounds) (M,T,W,Th,F,S)
  c. Shadow Boxing - 3 Rounds ** (daily)
  d. Muscle stretching - (daily)
  e. Heavy Bag - 3 Rounds ** (daily)
  f. Double Ended Bag - 3 Rounds ** (daily)
  g. Upper cut Bag - 3 Rounds ** (daily)
  h. Speed Bag - 3 Rounds (daily)

** Throw all the punches and combinations you have already learned, concentrating on your form.

. Conditioning Training (Something every day)

a. Weight training 2 days (M & Th) — (approximate time10 minutes)
For each exercise, you first have to determine the maximum amount of weight you are able to move

Part 2: Daily Practice Sessions at the Gym

just once. This is called your one repetition maximum (one "rep max"). The weight you should use for each exercise is 50% of your one repetition maximum. This is called 50% of your one "rep max". Therefore, you do all your exercises at 50% of your one "rep max". Do 3 sets of 8 repetitions ("reps") with 1 minute rest between sets. As a beginner, speak to your coach, and you may start with 3 sets of 4 reps and work up to 8 reps for each set.

1) Clean and press – Straight bar weight
2) Lateral shoulder raises – Dumbbell weight
3) Front lateral raises - Dumbbell weight 4) Rear lateral raises - Dumbbell weight

b. Plyometric training 2 days-(T & F)

1) Purpose: The purpose of plyometric training is to develop speed and explosiveness.

2) Exercises: 3 sets performed until "loss of explosiveness" with a 1 minute rest between sets. These exercises are performed only 2 days a week (T,F)

    a) Shoulders/arms on Tuesdays
        (1) Push-ups with 1 box
        (2) Push-ups with 2 boxes
        (3) Alternate push-ups with 2 boxes
        (4) Straight arm push-ups with 2 boxes
    b) Legs on Fridays
        (1) Vertical box jumps
        (2) Lateral box jumps left leg
        (3) Lateral box jumps right leg

c. Core Training Daily (Something every day)

1) Purpose: Your core must be strong to enable you to "take" a punch and also to deliver a powerful punch.

2) Exercises

    a) Roman Chair - lower core 3 sets of 15 – (every day)
    b) Decline sit-up bench – upper core 3 sets of 15 – (M,W, F)
    c) Medicine ball roll - 3 Sets of 1 minute with a 1 minute rest between sets – (T,Th,S)

d. Cardio-Respiratory (Heart-Lungs) Training 4 days (M,T,Th & F)

1) Exercises: 3 rounds for each with a 1 minute rest between rounds

    a) Boxes with dumbbell weights **(M & Th)** Use 3 pound weights performing each exercise for 30 seconds totaling 3 minutes for 1 round and 1 minute between rounds

        (1) Uppercuts for 30 seconds
        (2) Jabs for 30 seconds
        (3) Shoulder press for 30 seconds

    (4) Triceps for 30 seconds

    (5) Iron Cross for 30 seconds

    (6) Front extension hold for 30 seconds

b) Multi-directional runs – **(T)** Run for 3 rounds - 1 minute rest between rounds

c) Stair climbing – **(F)** Climb (up and down) for 3 rounds - 1 minute rest between rounds

Part 3: Lessons for the Right-Handed Boxer

PART 3: LESSONS FOR THE <u>RIGHT-HANDED BOXER</u>

1. Essential Human Anatomy for Boxers

As a boxer, you must understand the location of some essential body parts such as the STERNUM (breastbone) located in the MIDDLE of the upper chest, the HEART located on the LEFT SIDE of the upper chest under the ribs. The LIVER is under the lower ribs on the RIGHT SIDE of the body. The "SOLAR PLEXUS" is located in the upper abdomen (stomach area) just below the rib cage. Punches landing in the area of the heart, liver, floating ribs or "solar plexus" can cause severe pain. The floating ribs, numbers 11 and 12, are not attached to the sternum. (Figure 1)

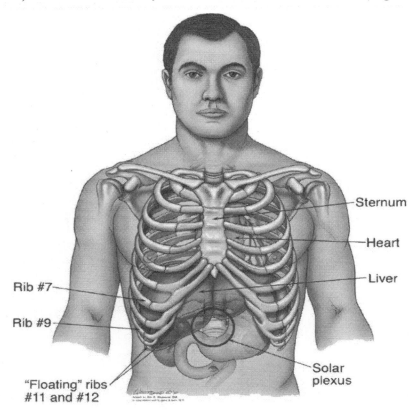

2. Introduction VIDEO CLIPS

a. Newton's Second Law of Motion, Weight Transfer and a Forceful Punch

A powerful punch is based on the science of physics and the laws of motion. Power punching requires understanding Newton's Second Law of Motion which is summarized and simplified by the formula $F=MA$. In the formula, F (force of your punch) is equal to your M (mass or your body weight) times A (acceleration or speed). Since your body weight is constant, to increase the force of your punch you must be able to accelerate (speed up) your movements. Therefore, a powerful, forceful punch comes from your ability to transfer your body weight rapidly combined with fast arm and fist motion. In other words, the ability to transfer your body weight from one place to another rapidly with a fast punching motion, generates the forceful, powerful punch. The moment of impact is called: The Moment of Maximum Force (MMF).

b. Stance (Boxing Position, Fighting Position, Set Position or Set)
The Foundation of the Buffalo System

Your Stance is also called your Boxing Position or Fighting Position, Set Position, or just Set. You can use these terms interchangeably. The Stance is the starting point or foundation for "building a boxer." Learning and then knowing your own particular Stance or Set Position is the essential foundation, which must be INGRAINED into your body so it can be assumed almost as a reflex, at any moment. EVERYTHING you do, your footwork and your forceful, powerful punches begin with your Stance or Set Position. From this position, you are "Set" to move rapidly (explosively) with your footwork, therefore you are "Set" on offense to move and punch forcefully with dynamic, explosive transfer of your entire body weight. You are also "Set" to defend yourself and counter punch when necessary.

c. Boxing off your Back Foot

Boxing off your back foot is essential to your ability to transfer your entire body weight (mass) from your back foot to your front foot, then from the front foot to the back foot which allows you to produce powerful, forceful punch with a STRAIGHT RIGHT or a LEFT HOOK. It is that rapid transfer of your body weight (mass) that is essential to the Buffalo System of power punching. By boxing off the back foot you are also able to transfer or drive your weight (mass) forward WITHOUT transferring your weight from your back foot to your front foot when you throw the LEFT JAB.

d. The LEFT JAB

When throwing your LEFT JAB, explosive motion of your left arm forward combined with explosive movement of your body weight (mass) forward generates the forceful, powerful punch and this is possible WITHOUT transferring your weight from your back foot to your front foot. By doing the lessons, you will learn how to throw a LEFT JAB correctly and transfer or drive your weight (mass) forward WITHOUT transferring your weight from your back foot to your front foot when you throw the LEFT JAB.

e. The STRAIGHT RIGHT (Power Punch # 1)

Your first power punch is The STRAIGHT RIGHT. The rapid (explosive) transfer of your body weight (mass) from the back foot to the front foot generates the power. In other words, it is the rapid (explosive) movement of your entire body forward from the back foot to the front foot that generates the tremendous force of your STRAIGHT RIGHT punch. The point of maximum impact is termed MMF (Moment of Maximum Force). The faster you move your mass (your body weight) the greater the force of your punch! By throwing a STRAIGHT RIGHT correctly, you transfer your entire body weight from your back foot to your front foot.

f. The LEFT HOOK (Power Punch #2)

After throwing your STRAIGHT RIGHT, your entire body weight transfers from your back foot to the front foot. With your body weight over your front foot, you can now throw a powerful LEFT HOOK. The LEFT HOOK, when thrown correctly, rapidly (explosively) transfers your entire body weight backwards from the front foot to the back foot.

In summary, fast (rapid and explosive) transfer of your body weight is essential to generate a forceful punch. For a forceful STRAIGHT RIGHT, you must rapidly transfer your body weight from your back foot to your front foot. For a forceful LEFT HOOK, you must rapidly transfer your body weight from

Part 3: Lessons for the Right-Handed Boxer

your front foot to your back foot. Therefore, a forceful, powerful punch requires the coordinated and balanced transfer of body weight. When throwing your LEFT JAB, fast motion of your left arm forward combined with fast movement of your body weight (mass) forward generates the forceful, powerful punch and this is possible WITHOUT transferring your weight from your back foot to your front foot. By mastering these lessons, you will learn how to throw the first three essential punches correctly with power.

g. Balance and awareness of your Body Weight Location

Successful development of boxing skills begins with the awareness of your Body Weight Location and its influence on your balance. You cannot box and punch effectively if you are off balance, and it is the awareness of your Body Weight Location that helps you understand balance. By doing the lessons, you will understand Body Weight Location, also called Body Weight Distribution and Balance.

All of the following lessons are building blocks, where each lesson progresses and builds upon the previous lesson. Study and master each lesson (building block) before progressing onto the next building block (lesson); otherwise, a flawed and imperfect boxer results. So, let's begin.

3. **Lesson 1: Balance and awareness of your Body Weight Location (distribution)—Related to the position of your chin**

As a boxer, you must understand that a powerful, forceful punch comes from transferring every ounce of your total body weight with every punch thrown at a fast speed. You must be able to "transfer every ounce of your total body weight with every punch you throw!"

As a new boxer, the first essential skill you must fully understand is the location of your total body weight so you can learn how to quickly, rapidly and explosively transfer that full body weight with each of your first three essential punches. The position of your chin determines where your weight is distributed.

Understanding the location and distribution of your body weight is essential in order to quickly transfer that body weight effectively. To understand your body weight distribution, first straddle one of the lines painted on the floor. (3-1) When your chin is placed directly over your right foot, it's impossible to lift your right foot without moving your chin because your entire body weight is over the right foot making it impossible to lift that right foot. (3-2)

3-1 When straddling a floor line the distribution of your weight is between your legs evenly distributed on both feet. You can't move either foot without moving your chin. The position of your chin determines the location of your body weight. Your CENTERLINE is an imaginary vertical line (vertical axis) starting at the top of your head extending down between your eyes and going further down between your legs.

3-2 By lifting your left foot, moving your chin to the right of your CENTERLINE it is now impossible to lift your right foot.

40

Part 3: Lessons for the Right-Handed Boxer

3-3 By lifting your right foot, moving your chin left of your CENTERLINE it is now impossible to lift your left foot.

The same holds true when you place your chin over your left foot. (3-3) You are unable to lift your foot without moving your chin. Your chin position (location) determines your Body Weight Location. Total awareness of the location and distribution of your body weight is the first step in building a boxer so that eventually you will be able to develop powerful, forceful punches by transferring every ounce of your total body weight with every punch you throw at very fast speeds.

4. Lesson 2: Stance (Boxing Position, Fighting Position, Set Position or Set)

Once you understand the location and distribution of your body weight, the next essential is establishing your own individual Stance, Boxing Position, also called Fighting Position, Set Position or Set.

Set Position or Set for short, is the foundation or platform on which a boxer is built. (3-4) From Set Position you can do almost EVERYTHING in boxing. You can move rapidly with your footwork and punch effectively on offense or block your opponent's punches on defense. Learning your own Set Position is essential since everything you do in boxing begins with your Stance (also called Boxing Position, Fighting Position, Set Position or just Set.)

a. Your Feet

Stand with your feet about shoulder width apart on each side of a floor line. The right foot is on the right side of the floor line, and the left foot is on the left side of the line each at a 45-degree angle to the line. Raise the heel of your back foot off the ground so you can move quickly. Slightly bend your knees. (3-4)

b. Your Hands

Position the right hand with the thumb resting against the right side of your face (jaw--chin) protecting it. Your right forearm should be resting against your rib cage protecting the ribs and the underlying liver, which is on the right side under the ribs. (3-4). The left hand is approximately 10 to 12 inches (2 fists) in front of the face just under the left eye. The thumb of both hands should be facing upwards. It is essential that your chin is "tucked in" below your shoulders. Your left shoulder points forward at your opponent's chest or your reflection in the mirror. Roll your upper back and shoulders to the right placing the chin on the right side of the line with the chin lining up just forward of the back or right foot. (3-4)

Your own individual stance, also called Boxing Position, Fighting Position or Set for the Right-Handed Boxer. Note the position of the chin, hands, elbows, knees and feet with the body weight distributed over the back foot behind your CENTERLINE. The heel of the back foot is off the floor.

Part 3: Lessons for the Right-Handed Boxer

c. Your Body Weight

Feel that your body weight is on the balls of your feet. The majority of your body weight must be distributed over the ball of the back foot, which is behind your CENTERLINE. Your CENTERLINE is an imaginary vertical line (vertical axis) starting at the top of your head extending down between your eyes and going further down between your legs, evenly distributing the weight over each foot. When your chin is behind your CENTERLINE your body weight is distributed or located over your back foot and conversely when your chin is in front of your CENTERLINE your body weight is distributed or located over your front foot. Now you have assumed your Stance, Fighting Position, Boxing Position, Set Position or Set. (3-4) Check your Stance with your coach and in the mirror. From this essential Set Position, you can do almost everything in boxing. You are set to move in any direction with your footwork and deliver your punches on offense or protect yourself on defense. When in your Stance be sure to feel that your body weight is behind your CENTERLINE with the majority of your body weight distributed or located over the ball of your back or rear foot in your Stance. This is exactly how you want to feel. Weight distributed behind your CENTERLINE over your back foot in your Stance. This is your Fighting Position, Boxing Position or Set Position. You **MUST** ask your coach to check your stance **BEFORE** you continue with the next lesson.

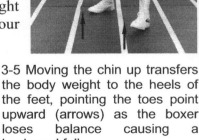

5. Lesson 3: Balance and Loss of Balance

In boxing, you **always** begin in your Stance, Boxing Position, Fighting Position, Set Position or Set. Your Stance is your foundation position. You must feel balanced in that Stance. As the boxer moves the chin upward, the body weight transfers to the heels of the feet, Of course, you must always AVOID losing your balance (3-5)

3-5 Moving the chin up transfers the body weight to the heels of the feet, pointing the toes point upward (arrows) as the boxer loses balance causing a backward fall.

6. Lesson 4: Essential Footwork-Learning to Box off Your Back Foot

a. Movement Forward

Practice this lesson in front of a mirror using the floor lines. Always begin in Set Position. (3-6) Start at one end of the line and move toward the mirror. When you reach the mirror at the end of the line, just walk back to the starting line and begin again. Always begin in your Stance, Boxing Position (Set Position). (3-6) Boxers move by opening their Stance and closing it. Learn to move out of Set Position and back into Set Position. Every second step will put you, the boxer, back into Boxing Position (Set Position). Move forward by pushing or driving off the ball of the back foot, moving the front foot forward (**about 6 inches**), "opening" or widening the Stance. (3-7) Then close the Stance by sliding the back foot forward, re-assuming Set Position. (3-8) The boxer's front foot meets the floor toes first. **DO NOT** meet the floor heel first because this will put you in an unbalanced position. A boxer **always** moves on the balls of the feet. The boxer's body weight MUST always be on the balls of the feet. The heel of the boxer's back foot remains approximately **ONE INCH OFF THE FLOOR** throughout this lesson.

3-6 Stance (Set Position) viewed from the side.

3-7 **MOVING FORWARD** by pushing off the ball of the back foot (opening the Stance) and driving the front foot forward.

3-8 Sliding the back foot forward (arrow) closing the Stance back into a new Set Position.

In order to transfer your weight and punch with power, you MUST learn to move with your footwork, while still maintaining your body weight (mass) over your back foot. While moving forward, the challenge is maintaining your body weight primarily over the back foot, by keeping your chin, rear or behind your own body CENTERLINE. Start this movement forward until you reach the end of a line about 30 feet (10 yards) away. Then walk back to the starting line and repeat, moving forward still maintaining your body weight over the back foot, rear of your own body CENTERLINE.

The coach is present for this lesson, and once you can consistently open and close your Stance and consistently return to Boxing Position (Set Position) going forward maintaining your weight behind or rear of your CENTERLINE over your back foot, you are ready for the next lesson. Accomplishing this lesson and finally feeling natural and comfortable with your Boxing Position (Stance, Set Position) and your body weight distributed behind your CENTERLINE over your back foot may require several days of daily practice. **Again, you may require SEVERAL DAYS of daily practice to master this lesson but do not proceed to the next lesson until you master maintaining your body weight over your back foot behind (rear) of your CENTERLINE. Unless you master this lesson you will be a flawed boxer and unable to perform the essential explosive footwork movements and the power punching skills with sustained efficiency to become a champion. You must learn to move in all directions while maintaining your weight rear of your CENTERLINE. As a boxer you MUST have the ability to transfer your body weight (mass) with your JAB still maintaining your body weight rear of the CENTERLINE on your back foot. For your STRAIGHT RIGHT you must be able to transfer your body weight through the CENTERLINE from your back foot to your front foot that is where your power of your STRAIGHT RIGHT comes from, that transfer of your body weight through the CENTERLINE. Alternately to develop the power of your LEFT HOOK you must be able to rapidly transfer the body weight from the front foot to the back foot again transferring your entire body weight from the front foot to the back foot through the CENTERLINE. This lesson must be MASTERED before progressing to the next lesson.**

Part 3: Lessons for the Right-Handed Boxer

b. Movement Backward

Perform this next lesson in front of the mirror with floor lines and always start in Boxing Position (Set Position). (3-9) Move backward by pushing or driving off the ball of your front foot, opening your Stance by pushing the back foot back about 6 inches. (3-10) Then slide the front foot back to Boxing Position (Set Position). (3-11) Your body weight MUST remain centered over the back foot at all times when moving forward and backward.

3-9 Start in Set Position.

3-10 **MOVING BACKWARD** by pushing off the ball of the front foot (opening the Stance) and driving the back foot backward. (arrow)

3-11 Sliding the front foot backward (arrow) closing the Stance back into a new Set Position.

c. Movement to Right and Left

This lesson is done in front of the mirror with floor lines and always starts in Boxing Position (Set Position). (3-12) You ALWAYS push off the foot opposite to the direction you intend to move.

1) Moving to the Right

The boxer moves to the RIGHT by pushing off the LEFT FOOT. (313) The boxer then slides the left foot back to Boxing Position (Set Position). (3-14) You always begin in Boxing Position then move in the desired direction and always return to Boxing Position (Set Position). You must always look exactly the same in your Boxing Position (Set Position) before starting a movement and after completing a movement.

2) Moving to the Left

The boxer begins in Boxing Position (Set Position). (3-15) The boxer moves to the LEFT by pushing off the RIGHT FOOT. (3-16) The boxer then slides the right foot back to Boxing Position (Set Position). (3-17) Once you can consistently move forward, backward and laterally to both the right and left while consistently maintaining Boxing Position (Set Position) with your body weight positioned over your back foot, you are ready for the coach's drill.

3-13 **MOVING TO THE RIGHT** (arrow) by pushing off the ball of the opposite (left) foot.

3-14 Sliding your left foot (arrow) to the right back into Set Position.

3-15 Start in Set Position.

3-16 **MOVING TO THE LEFT** (arrow) by pushing off the ball of the opposite right foot.

3-17 Sliding your right foot (arrow) to the left back into the Set Position.

The Coach's Drill

Have your coach stand in front of you and point in the direction you must move. You **MUST** be able to change directions quickly on the balls of your feet keeping your body weight over your back foot. The toes of your shoes must not leave the floor when you are in Boxing Position (Set Position). If the front of your shoes or toes rises off the floor, you are off balance; and loss of balance must always be avoided.

Part 3: Lessons for the Right-Handed Boxer

7.   **Lesson 5: Essential Footwork "Step-and-a-Half"**

This lesson is done in front of the mirror with the floor lines and always starts in Boxing Position (Set Position). (3-18) This lesson helps you understand rapid (explosive) footwork movement and range.   Boxers must **NEVER LUNGE** or take large steps. You must take small steps moving explosively (powerfully) from Boxing Position (Set Position) and back into Boxing Position (Set Position) while always maintaining balance in your proper Stance with the body weight distributed over the back foot. The purpose of "Step-and-a-Half" is to move rapidly (explosively) into a new position and closing range (getting closer to an opponent) to punch effectively, without lunging.

3-18 Start in Set Position.

a. Forward

To accomplish "Step-and-a-Half" forward, the boxer first steps forward (3-19) and then hops forward (3-20) by pushing off the back foot and landing on his back foot first in Boxing Position (Set Position). (3-21)

Once you are able to perform "Step-and-a-Half" consistently forward, you must also learn to go backward.

3-19 "STEP AND-A-HALF" FORWARD Stepping forward first.

3-20 Then hopping forward landing on the back foot first. (arrows)

3-21 Back into Set Position.

b. Backward

Start in Boxing Position (Set Position) (3-22) Push off the front foot (3-23) and stepping with back foot and then hopping (3-24) backward into Boxing Position (Set Position). (3-25)

3-21 Start in Set Position	3-23 **"STEP AND-A-HALF" BACKWARD** Stepping backward first. (arrow)	3-24 Then hopping backward landing on the front foot first. (arrow)	3-21 Back in Set Position.

c. To The Right

This lesson starts in Boxing Position (Set Position). (3-26) To take a "Step-and-a-Half" to the right, the boxer steps to the right by pushing off the left foot (3-27) and hops (3-28) to the right landing on the front foot first back into Boxing Position. (Set Position). (3-29)

3-26 Start in Set Position.	3-27 **"STEP AND-A-HALF" TO THE RIGHT** Stepping to the right first. (arrow)	3-28 Hopping to the right landing on the front foot first. (arrows)	3-26 Back into Set Position.

Part 3: Lessons for the Right-Handed Boxer

d. To The Left

The boxer starts in Boxing Position (Set Position). (3-30) To take a "Step-and-a-Half" to the left, the boxer steps to the left and pushes off his right foot (3-31) opening his Stance to the left landing on the back foot first and hops (3-32) to left back into Set Position (Boxing Position). (3-33)

3-30 Start in Set Position.

3-31 **"STEP AND-A-HALF" TO THE LEFT** Stepping to the left first.(arrow)

3-32 Hopping to the left landing on the back foot first. (arrow)

3-33 Back into Set Position.

8. Lesson 6:

Essential Footwork--The "Pivot"

Perform this lesson in front of the mirror with floor lines and always start in Boxing Position (Set Position). (3-34) The "Pivot" is the first essential step to understanding angles. The boxer pivots or spins one quarter turn or 90 degrees clockwise (rotating on the front left foot with your head and body TURNING to your RIGHT) on the ball of the front foot while maintaining Boxing Position (Set Position). (3-35) Practice The "Pivot" clockwise 90 degrees (rotating on your front left foot) turning 4 times until you are back to the beginning in Boxing Position (Set Position). Now pivot in the opposite direction by starting in Boxing Position (Set Position) and pivot (3-36) a quarter turn or 90 degrees counter-clockwise (rotating on your front left foot with your head and body TURNING to your LEFT) on the ball of the front foot while maintaining Boxing Position (Set Position). (3-37) Next practice The "Pivot" counterclockwise 4 times until you are back to starting position. You must be able to pivot clockwise (rotating to the right) and pivot counter-clockwise (rotating to the left) before going on to the next lesson.

3-34 Start in Set Position.

3-35 **PIVOT CLOCKWISE** (turning to your right) on the ball of your front (left) foot (arrow shows boxer facing new direction after a clockwise pivot)

3-36 Start in Set Position

3-37 **PIVOT COUNTER CLOCKWISE** (turning to your left) on the ball of your front (left) foot (arrow shows boxer facing new direction after a counter clockwise pivot)

9. Lesson 7: Essential Footwork--The "Step Around" (Step and Pivot)

Perform this lesson in front of the mirror with floor lines and always start in Boxing Position (Set Position). (3-38) The "Step Around" is a small step to the left with the left foot (3-39) followed by a pivot clockwise (3-40) on that left foot with your head and body TURNING to your RIGHT. The "Step Around" (Step and Pivot) to the left develops an angle to the opponent's right.

3-38 Start in Set Position

3-39 The **STEP AROUND**
Step to the left (arrow)
and pivot clockwise
(turning to your right)

3-40 Pivot clockwise (turning to the right) on the ball of your front (left) foot (arrows shows boxer facing a new direction after a clockwise pivot). It is the Step with The "Pivot" that defines the "Step Around" which changes to the angle 90 degrees)

10. Lesson 8: Essential Footwork- The "Scissor Step"

Perform this lesson in front of the mirror with floor lines and always start in Boxing Position (Set Position). (3-41) The "Scissor Step" is the quickest way for a Right-Handed Boxer to move laterally to the right. The boxer opens the Stance equally and in opposite directions (3-42) and then slides the left foot back to Boxing Position (Set Position). (3-43)

3-41 Start in Set Position

3-42 **"SCISSORS STEP"**
Opening the Stance equally in
opposite directions (arrows going to
the left and right at the same time.)

3-43 Sliding the left foot
(arrow) back into Set
Position resulting in
movement to the right.

Part 3: Lessons for the Right-Handed Boxer

11. **Lesson 9: Rhythm:**
Rhythm is the flow or movement of rocking back and forth in Boxing Position (Set Position).

You **MUST** ask your coach to check your Essential Footwork and Rhythm (Lessons 5-9) **BEFORE** you continue with the next lesson, the **LEFT JAB**.

12. **Lesson 10: The LEFT JAB**

Perform this lesson in front of the mirror with the floor lines and always start in Boxing Position (Set Position). The LEFT JAB is the boxer's most important punch. The Jab helps determine the distance or range to the opponent. By using the Jab, you can break or disrupt the opponent's rhythm. The LEFT JAB prepares the boxer to throw the right hand power punch. The boxer assumes Boxing Position (Set Position) on the lines in front of the mirror. (3-44) As soon as you start to throw the LEFT JAB, the left foot simultaneously steps forward and lands on the floor at exactly the same time as the left arm is fully extended. (3-45) Your upper torso turns and rolls to the right with the left shoulder resting against the left side of the jaw. The boxer must **EXHALE WHILE THROWING THE PUNCH**. As soon as the left arm is fully extended with the wrist turned over, the left arm retracts in a straight line back to Boxing Position (Set Position) as the right (back) foot moves forward. (3-46) The punch mechanics of the LEFT JAB begins as the boxer throws the LEFT JAB in a straight line from Boxing Position (Set Position) while turning the wrist and hand over so the boxer's knuckles are parallel to the floor with the wrist fixed in a straight line at the end of the punch. (3-47a and b) (3-48 and 49). The footwork for the Jab and associated weight transfer is such, that as the boxer initiates the LEFT JAB, the left front foot moves forward opening the Stance and as the wrist and hand turn over and as the arm fully extends, as the left front foot lands on the floor at the exact same time as the body weight transfers forward pushing off the back leg. The boxer's chin must remain behind the CENTER LINE or vertical axis, **STILL KEEPING THE BODY WEIGHT ON THE BACK RIGHT FOOT**. The back leg and boxer's left arm return to Boxing Position (Set Position) at the same time. The Jab is most effective when the arm is fully extended at the correct distance or range so that the punch lands on your opponent with your arm fully extended at the same time your front foot hits the floor after taking a small step. The Jab is similar to the stinging produced by snapping a towel. The maximum sting occurs when the towel is fully extended. The snapping towel is less effective at producing a sting when the range is shortened and the towel is too close to the subject. The same is true of the Jab. The Jab is most effective when it hits your opponent with your arm fully extended as your body weight and momentum transfers forward. The boxer should target the Jab to the opponent's eye since a jab in the eye will obscure vision and can tilt the opponent's head back. By tilting the opponent's head backward, the chin moves upward, causing the opponent's body weight to transfer backward the opponent losing balance. In addition, with the head tilting backward, the opponent's chin is vulnerable to your power punch, the STRAIGHT RIGHT hand, which can be thrown as your next punch. You **MUST** ask your coach to check your LEFT JAB **BEFORE** you continue with the next lesson.

3-44 Start in Set Position for The **LEFT** JAB.

3-45 **LEFT JAB** Exactly as the FRONT foot moves forward (arrow), the punching left arm moves forward. The upper body (torso) rolls to the right as the left shoulder rolls against the left side of the face (protecting the jaw-chin). The punch is fully extended as the front foot hits the floor.

34-6 LEFT JAB Exactly as the BACK foot slides forward (arrow), the punching left arm moves backward into Set Position.

3-47a

3-47b

3-48

3-49

3-47 a and b **LEFT JAB** With the boxer facing you, notice the turning of the wrist (3-48) and hand so the boxer's knuckles rotate and become parallel to the floor at the end of the punch (3-49) and the left shoulder protects the left side of the face (protecting the jaw-chin).

Part 3: Lessons for the Right-Handed Boxer

13. Lesson 11: Practicing Range

First practice the LEFT JAB in front of the mirror, and when the mechanics of the punch are mastered, and checked by your coach, you then practice the LEFT JAB on the heavy bag by starting in Boxing Position (Set Position). First touch the heavy bag with a fully extended left hand on the bag **WITHOUT** taking a step. (3-50) Then step back a half step (**about 6 inches**) with the back right foot and then with the front left foot back into Boxing Position (Set Position). (3-51) Now take a small step (**about 6 inches**) forward to hit the bag. (3-52) This is the boxer's RANGE. This is your range. Practice the Jab on the heavy bag by hitting the bag in the middle of the swing as the bag comes toward you. You should time the punch so the Jab hits the bag with the arm fully extended ("locked out") while taking a small step forward. You are too close to the bag if as the bag is hit, the bag is pushed forward causing it to swing. The bag will make a popping sound when it is hit at the correct range, causing the bag to stop swinging. The boxer's head should **NEVER** be directly in front of the bag when the Jab strikes the bag. With a correctly thrown LEFT JAB, your head and upper torso must roll to your right with the left shoulder rolling against the jaw, protecting the jaw, placing the head slightly to the right of the bag. Now you will start to understand range.

3-50 Practicing the **LEFT JAB** on the heavy bag, first by touching the bag with the left hand in Set Position.

3-51 Next with both feet take a small step back (about 6 inches) back (arrow) away from the bag with both the front and back feet returning to Set Position.

3-52 **LEFT JAB** Taking a small step (about 6 inches) forward (arrow) to hit the bag, this is the boxer's range. Strike the bag as it swings back toward you. Hit the bag in the middle of the swing. When hit correctly, a popping sound occurs as the bag stops swinging.

Your timing is correct when you strike the bag with the LEFT JAB at the center of its swing (causing the bag to stop) just as your left foot hits the floor. Your range is correct when the bag is struck with your LEFT JAB after taking a small step with the left arm fully extended or "locked out." You must time the landing of your punch as your front left foot hits the floor. Every punch should set up another punch. The LEFT JAB sets up The STRAIGHT RIGHT. The LEFT JAB must be practiced in front of the mirror and on the heavy bag until all aspects of the mechanics and breathing are mastered, remembering to **EXHALE** while throwing each punch. Once range is understood and reproduced in front of your coach, you may then "dance" with the bag and practice your LEFT JAB with a moving heavy bag. You **MUST** ask your coach to check your RANGE **BEFORE** you continue with the next lesson.

14. Lesson 12: Dancing with the bag (reinforcing footwork) at range

The coach pushes the heavy bag so it swings forward and backward in a straight line. The boxer is told to move back and forth keeping the bag at range with the essential footwork already learned. Use your footwork, keeping the heavy bag in range at all times so you can take that small step striking the heavy bag with your fully extended LEFT JAB. Next the coach pushes the heavy bag side-to-side, and the boxer moves laterally to the right and left, keeping the bag at range. The coach next pushes the bag in different directions with the boxer using the essential footwork, maintaining Boxing Position (Set Position) in front of the heavy bag at range and striking the bag with the LEFT JAB on command by the coach. After this is mastered, you can work with the heavy bag on your own, pushing the heavy bag in different directions and staying in range striking the bag with the LEFT JAB, remembering to **EXHALE** while throwing the LEFT JAB.

15. Lesson 13: Dancing with the bag--The "Pivot" (The First Angle) at range

Now the boxer learns to keep the bag at range using The "Pivot" (The First Angle). The boxer hits the bag with the LEFT JAB and then pivots. The boxer must practice The Jab and "Pivot" while returning to Boxing Position (Set Position) in front of the heavy bag at range. As the coach changes the bag's direction, the boxer moves on the balls of the feet, opening and closing Boxing Position (Set Position) returning to Boxing Position with every second step. The coach must observe and always correct the boxer's footwork to be sure the footwork is performed correctly. Practice The "Pivot", staying in range so you can hit the swinging bag with your LEFT JAB.

16. Lesson 14: Dancing with the bag--The "Step Around" (Step and Pivot) (The Second Angle) at range

The coach pushes the heavy bag, and when the bag reaches the center of its swing, the boxer throws the LEFT JAB then takes a first step to the left and pivots to be in position to hit the bag again with a fully extended LEFT JAB. Practice the "Step Around" (Step and Pivot) to the left, staying in range so you can hit the swinging bag with your LEFT JAB.

17. Lesson 15: Dancing with the bag--The "Scissor Step" at range

The boxer practices The "Scissors Step" to the right to be in position to hit the bag with a fully extended LEFT JAB at range.

18. Lesson 16: The STRAIGHT RIGHT (Power Punch One)

Standing in front of the mirror with the floor lines start in Boxing Position (Set Position). The STRAIGHT RIGHT is a power or "knockout" punch. In order to throw this punch correctly, you must be able to transfer your body weight from the back foot to the front foot. The boxer starts in Boxing Position (Set Position). (3-53) The boxer will transfer body weight from the back foot to the front foot by turning (pivoting) on the toe (ball) of the right foot moving the heel to the right or counter-clockwise as the boxer's body weight transfers from the back foot to the front foot. (3-54) Note: As the chin passes through the boxer's CENTERLINE to the front foot, this movement forces the shoulders and hips to "square up." (3-55) The boxer's feet will be spaced the same distance apart as they were in Boxing Position (Set Position). The boxer's knee over the front leg will bend slightly as the back foot pivots, placing the chin directly over the front knee and over the toe of the front foot. (3-56) This is called the "3-Point Line-Up":
1) The point of the chin
2) The point of the knee, and
3) The point of the toe.

3-53 Start in Set Position for The **STRAIGHT RIGHT.**

3-54   **STRAIGHT RIGHT**
The boxer transfers the body weight from the back foot to the front foot as the chin moves through the CENTERLINE and the "3-Point Line-Up" is achieved. The 3 points from (top to bottom) are: 1) the chin 2) the front (left) knee and 3) the toe of the front (left) foot.

3-55 As the **STRAIGHT RIGHT** is thrown, with the weight transfer from the back foot to the front foot, the chin passes through the CENTERLINE and the hips and shoulders are "squared up" (hips and shoulders facing directly forward). The heel of the right foot is elevated with the **STRAIGHT RIGHT**.

3-56 **STRAIGHT RIGHT** Note the "3 Point Line Up" of the chin, left knee and the left toe.

Therefore, the chin and knee are lined up directly over the toe of the front foot. By bending the knee ("sitting down on the punch"), the boxer transfers the body weight to the ball of the front foot while maintaining balance. Before the punch is thrown, the boxer's head and chin are positioned rear of the CENTERLINE and just in front of the back (right) foot, with the body weight over the back (right) foot. After the punch is thrown, the chin and the body weight is transferred over the front (left) foot. When the boxer finishes bending the knee or "sitting down on the punch", the body weight drops straight down toward the floor. "Sitting down on the punch" allows a boxer to control his or her own inertia. By dropping the body weight straight down toward the floor, the boxer's balance is maintained as the body weight transfers from the back foot to the front foot, keeping the boxer from falling forward and losing balance.

The STRAIGHT RIGHT starts on the right side of the boxer's chin with the elbow resting against the rib cage. The right elbow and the right hip rotate or turn through the punch together. The right arm should lie against the boxer's rib cage all the way through the punch. The right shoulder should come to rest against the right side of the boxer's face, protecting the boxer from a counter punch while protecting the jaw. The fast twitch muscles used to throw this punch are primarily the anterior deltoid muscles (one of the muscles that form the rounded contour of the shoulder). The STRAIGHT RIGHT should be aimed at your opponent's chin. You must **EXHALE** as the punch is thrown and retract your arm as quickly as possible back into Boxing Position (Set Position). You **MUST** ask your coach to check your STRAIGHT RIGHT **BEFORE** you continue with the next lesson.

19. Lesson 17: The First Combination—Two punches (LEFT JAB and a STRAIGHT RIGHT)

Each punch (when thrown correctly) will "Set Up" or prepare you to throw another punch. The LEFT JAB "sets up" The STRAIGHT RIGHT. The First Combination that every right-handed boxer learns is The LEFT JAB followed by a STRAIGHT RIGHT. You always start in Boxing Position (Set Position). (3-53) The boxer opens the stance with the LEFT JAB fully extended to determine range. (3-57) The boxer then closes the stance while moving (pivoting) the right foot counter-clockwise, "pushing" the ball of the right foot forward which simulates "squishing" or "squeezing" a bug into the floor. (3-58) The boxer's feet should be shoulder width apart, approximating Set Position, maintaining balance after bringing the right foot forward. If the front foot moves forward 3 inches, the back foot comes forward 3 inches, returning the boxer to Boxing Position (Set Position). When throwing the LEFT JAB, your left shoulder will rest against the left side of your face while your torso will roll to the right. Now when throwing The STRAIGHT RIGHT, your right shoulder will rest against the right side of your face while your body rolls to the left with the chin stopping directly over the left knee, which must line up directly over the left front foot in

3-58 The **STRAIGHT RIGHT**. Note the right shoulder protecting the jaw on the right side and "3-Point Line-Up" with the chin, the left knee and the toe of the left foot in a straight line. The right foot has moved slightly forward and rotated counter- clockwise pointing the toes forward as the right arm and hand are extended rapidly at exactly the same time as the weight transfer from the back foot (heel elevated) to the front foot reaching the Moment of Maximum Force (MMF) for that punch. The faster the weight is transferred from the back foot to the front foot the greater the force of the punch, obeying Newton's Second Law (F=MA) where the force of the punch F is increased by weight (M or mass) transfer multiplied by the speed of the punch (A or acceleration or simplified as speed of the punch).The **STRAIGHT RIGHT** sets up the **LEFT HOOK** since the **STRAIGHT RIGHT** ends with all the weight on the front left foot in the "3-Point Line-Up".

3-53 Start in Set Position for the **STRAIGHT RIGHT**

3-57 The left jab sets up straight right.

3-58

Part 3: Lessons for the Right-Handed Boxer

The LEFT JAB should be aimed at the opponent's eye, obstructing vision and causing the opponent's chin to move up and back, redistributing the opponent's weight to the heels of the feet throwing the opponent off balance. The STRAIGHT RIGHT should be aimed at the opponent's chin for the "knockout"!

A boxer must <u>NEVER</u> move straight back after throwing a STRAIGHT RIGHT. A boxer moving straight back is vulnerable to being hit by either of the opponent's hands. The "Bump" (Dip and Hop) to the right is used after The STRAIGHT RIGHT is thrown. The "Bump" is used to establish an angle (or "break" an angle) out of your opponent's range but still in your range. The "Bump" (Dip and Hop) to the right after throwing a STRAIGHT RIGHT places your body weight on your back foot. The right leg must land on the floor directly under you as the floor stops your inertia. This allows you to avoid your opponent's offense by being out of the opponent's range, yet you are in position to throw another STRAIGHT RIGHT. You **MUST** ask your coach to check your FIRST COMBINATION **BEFORE** you continue with the next lesson.

20. Lesson 18: Practicing The First Combination (LEFT JAB, STRAIGHT RIGHT) on the Heavy Bag

Hit the heavy bag at range with a LEFT JAB as you step and as your head rolls to the right and outside th bag. Your head should NEVER stop directly in front of the bag. Next, you should immediately throw The STRAIGHT RIGHT closing the stance back into Boxing Position (Set Position) as the head rolls to the left and outside the bag. You MUST ask your coach to check your FIRST COMBINATION BEFORE you continue with the next lesson.

21. Lesson 19: The "Step Around" (Step and Pivot) to the left (The Second Angle) and The "Bump" (Dip and Hop) to the right (The Third Angle)

You must <u>NEVER</u> step straight back after throwing a STRAIGHT RIGHT hand; therefore, after throwing the LEFT JAB and STRAIGHT RIGHT combination, you can either "Bump" to the right or "Step Around" to the left. In either situation you move back into Boxing Position (Set Position), and you are in a position to punch again with another STRAIGHT RIGHT or another LEFT JAB without being punched.

The First Angle is the "Pivot". The Second Angle is the "Step Around" (Step and Pivot) to the left. The Third Angle is the "Bump" (Dip and Hop) to the right. Developing angles allows you to be in an offensive position, to hit without being hit outside your opponent's right or left hand placing the opponent in a defensive position. The "Step Around" to your left renders the opponent's right and left hands useless, and the "Bump" to your right renders the opponent's left and right hands useless. If after throwing a punch you end up positioned outside the opponent's right shoulder, the best angle is the "Step Around" (Step and Pivot) to the left. On the other hand, if you are positioned outside the opponent's left hand, the best angle is the "Bump" (Dip and Hop) to the right, placing the opponent in a defensive position and closer to the opponent's left hand but you are in position to use The STRAIGHT RIGHT again. So caution is advised, and it is usually best for the Right-Handed Boxer to move counter-clockwise away from the opponent's powerful right hand; thus, after throwing the STRAIGHT RIGHT, it is usually best to "Bump" (Dip and Hop) (The Third Angle) counter-clockwise to your right and away from your opponent's power. You MUST ask your coach to check your "STEP AROUND" and "BUMP" after throwing the FIRST COMBINATION BEFORE you continue with the next lesson.

22. Lesson 20: The LEFT HOOK (Power Punch Two), (Short Range)

a. Footwork in front of mirror

The STRAIGHT RIGHT sets up the LEFT HOOK. The right hand ends with all of the boxer's weight on the ball of the front foot with the chin and knee lined up directly over the toes of the front foot in the "3-Point Line-Up". (3-58) The LEFT HOOK starts as the boxer rapidly turns both ankles clockwise (turning, facing to the right) 90 degrees, with the heel of his front foot off the ground and both knees slightly bent. This rapid turning of both feet transfers the entire body weight from the front foot to the back foot. The boxer's chin and right knee will now be directly over the toes of the right foot in the "3-Point Line-Up". (3-59) The boxer must keep the shoulders rounded with the chin tucked below and against the left shoulder, for defense and balance.

3-58 The **STRAIGHT RIGHT.** Note the right shoulder protecting the jaw on the right side and "3-Point-Line-Up with the chin, the left knee and the toe of the left foot in a straight line. The right foot has moved slightly forward and rotated counter-clockwise pointing the toes forward as the right arm and hand are extended rapidly at exactly the same time as the weight transfer from the back foot (heel elevated) to the front foot reaching the Moment of Maximum Force (MMF) for that punch. The faster the weight is transferred from the back foot to the front foot, the greater the force of the punch, obeying Newton's Second Law (F=MA) where the force of the punch F is increased by weight (M or mass) transfer multiplied by the speed of the punch (A or acceleration or simplified as speed of the punch). The **STRAIGHT RIGHT** sets up **the LEFT HOOK** since the STRAIGHT RIGHT ends with all the weight on the front left foot in the "3-Point Line-Up".

3-59 The **LEFT HOOK:** Note the left shoulder protecting the jaw on the left side and "3-Point-Line-Up" with the chin, the right knee and the toe of the right foot in a straight line. The left foot and the right foot have both rotated clockwise, pointing the toes 90 degreed to the right as the left arm and hand are extended rapidly at exactly the same time as the weight transfer from the front foot (heel elevated) to the back foot reaching the Moment of Maximum Force (MMF) for that punch. The faster the weight is transferred from the front foot to the back foot the greater the force of the punch, obeying Newtown's Second Law (F=MA) where the force of the punch F is increased by weight (M or mass) transfer (front foot to back foot) multiplied by the speed of the punch). Note also the heel of the front left foot is elevated with the LEFT HOOK and the heel of the right foot is elevated with The **STRAIGHT RIGHT.**

b. Punch Mechanics Short Range LEFT HOOK /Thumb pointing toward your face.

The LEFT HOOK can be thrown at different distances or ranges. The Short Range LEFT HOOK is delivered across the boxer's body with the left arm bent 90 degrees and parallel to the floor. (3-60) (3-61) The boxer's left shoulder will rest against the chin, providing defense. The MMF (Moment of Maximum Force) is generated at the end of the punch as it lands on the target and occurs just as the boxer transfers the entire body weight from the front foot to the back foot. You MUST ask your coach to check your LEFT HOOK BEFORE you continue with the next lesson.

3-60 **SHORT RANGE LEFT HOOK**
Close up of the left hand the thumb protecting the boxers face.

3-61 Side view of the **SHORT RANGE LEFT HOOK**: Note this Short Range LEFT Hook with the left shoulder protecting the left side of the face (jaw-chin) and the left arm and left forearm are at right angles to each other. The thumb of the left hand is pointing toward the boxer's face.

Part 3: Lessons for the Right-Handed Boxer

23. Lesson 21: LEFT HOOK (Power Punch Two), (Long Range)

a. Footwork in front of mirror

The footwork for the Long Range LEFT HOOK is exactly the same as the footwork for the Short Range LEFT HOOK with the transfer of body weight from the front foot to the back foot.

b. Punch Mechanics: Long Range LEFT HOOK/Thumb pointing upward

Changing a Short Range LEFT HOOK to a Long Range LEFT HOOK requires extending your left arm by rotating your wrist away from your face thereby changing the position of the thumb from pointing toward your face to the "thumbs up" position. As the LEFT HOOK extends 90 degrees, you start to "ratchet" or rotate the wrist away from your face or counter-clockwise causing the thumb to point further away from your face. A Long Range LEFT HOOK lands with the thumb pointing upwards. (3-62) (3-63) You **MUST** ask your coach to check your LONG RANGE LEFT HOOK **BEFORE** you continue with the next lesson.

3-62 **LONG RANGE LEFT HOOK** Close-up of the left hand with the thumb starting to rotate away from the boxer's face to a more thumb's up position.

3-63 Side view of the **LONG RANGE LEFT HOOK.**

24. Lesson 22: The Second Combination--Three Punches (LEFT JAB, STRAIGHT RIGHT and Short and Long Range LEFT HOOK)

a. Short Range

This Second Combination with the Short Range LEFT HOOK must also be practiced and mastered on the heavy bag. Set Position (3-64), LEFT JAB (3-65), STRAIGHT RIGHT (3-66), Short Range LEFT HOOK. (3-67)

3-64 Start in Set Position for the **SECOND COMBINATION** (LEFT JAB followed by The STRAIGHT RIGHT followed by the Short Range LEFT HOOK).

3-65 **LEFT JAB**

3-66 **STRAIGHT RIGHT**

3-67 **SHORT RANGE LEFT HOOK**

b. Long Range

This Second Combination with the Long Range LEFT HOOK must also be practiced and mastered on the heavy bag. Set Position (3-68), LEFT JAB (3-69), STRAIGHT RIGHT (3-70), Long Range LEFT HOOK (3-71) (3-72) You **MUST** ask your coach to check your SECOND COMBINATION with both you Short and Long Range LEFT HOOK.

3-68 Start in Set Position for the **SECOND COMBINATION** (LEFT JAB followed by The STRAIGHT RIGHT followed by the Long Range LEFT HOOK).

3-69 LEFT JAB

3-72 LONG RANGE LEFT HOOK Side View of the left hand with the thumb starting to rotate away from the boxer's face to a more "thumb's up" position.

3-70 STRAIGHT RIGHT

3-71 LONG RANGE LEFT

Part 3: Lessons for the Right-Handed Boxer

25. Lesson 23: Footwork Drills with 3 Angles

REMEMBER; NEVER finish a combination by moving straight back. It is essential to finish all your combinations by moving into a new position by developing angles (also termed "breaking an angle") so you can strike (punch) again without being hit. Therefore, it is essential that after any combination you move into a new position by developing an angle or "breaking an angle".

You must practice all three angles when working the heavy bag.
* 1. The First Angle is The "Pivot".
* 2. The Second Angle is The "Step Around" (Step and Pivot) to the **left.**
* 3. The Third Angle is The "Bump" (Dip and Hop) to the **right.**

Choosing the angle depends upon the position you are in after throwing a combination, and you may choose to use or develop any one of the three angles. For the Right-Handed Boxer, the best is the Third Angle which is the "Bump" (Dip and Hop) to the right after finishing the First Combination or the "Step Around" (Step and Pivot) after the Second Combination. If after throwing a punch, you end up positioned outside the opponent's right shoulder, the best angle is The "Step Around" (Step and Pivot) to your left, angling you away from the Right-Handed opponent's powerful right hand. Developing The Second Angle, The "Step Around" allows you to be in an offensive position outside the opponent's right hand placing the opponent in a defensive position. The Third Angle is the "Bump" (Dip and Hop) to the right rendering the opponent's left and right hands useless, allowing you to be in an offensive position outside the opponent's left hand placing the opponent in a defensive position.

After throwing The STRAIGHT RIGHT, you are in position to throw the LEFT HOOK because all of your weight is on the ball of the front foot. Remember to throw the LEFT HOOK, you turn both ankles to the right (clockwise) 90 degrees on the balls of the feet with the heel of the left (front) foot off the ground. Both knees should be slightly bent. This rapid movement will transfer all of your body weight to the back right (rear) foot, evenly distributing weight on the whole foot. Your chin, right knee, and the toes (front of the right foot) will "line-up" over each other in the "3-Point Line-Up".

It is essential that your shoulders are rounded with your chin tucked below and against the left shoulder for defense and balance. As the short LEFT HOOK is thrown, your left arm comes across your body with the left arm bent 90 degrees and parallel to the floor. The thumb of your left hand will be pointed toward your face with the knuckles in a straight line parallel to the floor. Your chin will rest against your left shoulder providing defense. Since the MMF (Moment of Maximum Force) of your LEFT HOOK occurs at the end of the punch, the punch should land on target just as your body weight transfers from the left (front) foot to the right (back) foot.

The LEFT HOOK can be thrown at various distances or ranges. The Short Range LEFT HOOK is thrown at a right angle or 90 degrees. To throw a Long Range LEFT HOOK, start to rotate your left wrist and fist away from your face, causing the thumb of your left hand to point further away from the face as this extends the reach of the LEFT HOOK. Now you **MUST** have your coach check all your punches, combinations, footwork and angles on the heavy bag so you can begin practicing and **MASTERING** these ESSENTIAL BOXING SKILLS **BEFORE** you begin "RING DRILLS" and Sparring.

Part 4: DVD 1 **VIDEO CLIPS FOR THE RIGHT-HANDED BOXER**

A. FUNDAMENTALS

B. "RING DRILLS" AND SPARRING

This part covers the Fundamentals and "Ring Drills" including introduction to sparring for the beginner (novice) Right-Handed Boxer. The novice will learn to perform these "Ring Drills" against both a Right-Handed Boxer and a Left-Handed Boxer on both offense and defense learning the following in detail. It will all be covered on the DVD (video clips) in detail on DVD 1. Be sure to study the summary of blocks and counter punches on Tables 4-1 and 4-2, page 64.

YOU WILL LEARN:
- How to throw the first 3 punches.
- How to throw the first 2 combinations.
- How to develop the essential 3 angles.
- How to defend against and block the first 3 punches.
- How to throw counter punches **AGAINST** a Right-Handed opponent.
- How to throw counter punches **AGAINST** a Left-Handed opponent.
- How to cut off the ring.
- How to fight off the ropes.
- How to fight out of a corner.

Part 4: DVD 1 (DVD) *VIDEO CLIPS for the Right-Handed Boxer*

AGAINST A RIGHT-HANDED BOXER

1. Introduction
   a. Newton's Second Law of Motion
   b. Stance
   c. Boxing off your Back Foot
   d. Essential Footwork
   e. Footwork drills with 3 Angles
      1) The "Pivot"
      2) The "Step Around" (Step and Pivot)
      3) The "Bump" (Dip and Hop)
2. Offense Practice throwing a LEFT JAB
   b. STRAIGHT RIGHT
   c. The First Combination
   d. LEFT HOOK
      1) Short Range
      2) Long Range
   e. The Second Combination
3. Purpose of Ring Drills: To allow the beginner to improve skills in the ring without the risk of being injured or hurt, "to teach not injure".

4. Position goals: Your **LEFT SHOULDER** should be facing your opponent's chest. Keep your opponent in front of you at ALL times. Move either clockwise or counter-clockwise, always maintaining your opponent directly in front of you.

5. Defense – Practice blocks/counter punches, after reading below about each block and each counter punch separately, DVD ONE shows the blocks and counter punches together. a. Blocks against LEFT JAB - open (palm) right hand block.
   b. Blocks against STRAIGHT RIGHT- left forearm block and turn ankles 90 degrees clockwise.
   c. Blocks against The First Combination - open (palm) right hand block, left forearm block and turn ankles 90 degrees clockwise.
   d. Blocks against LEFT HOOK - block with back of right hand.
   e. Blocks against The Second Combination - all 3 blocks.
   f. Counter punches against LEFT JAB - counter is a LEFT JAB.
   g. Counter punches against STRAIGHT RIGHT- counter is a STRAIGHT RIGHT.
   h. Counter punches against The First Combination - counter is a STRAIGHT RIGHT.
   i. Counter punches against LEFT HOOK - counter **depends** where your weight is distributed:
      1) If your weight is on your **back foot**, counter punch is a STRAIGHT RIGHT.
      2) If your weight is on your **front foot**, counter punch is a LEFT HOOK.
   j. Counter punches against The Second Combination - counter is:
      1) If your weight is on your **back foot**, counter punch is a STRAIGHT RIGHT.
      2) If your weight is on your **front foot**, counter punch is a LEFT HOOK.
6. Advanced footwork drills
   a. Cutting off the ring
   b. Fighting off the ropes
   c. Fighting out of a corner

Part 4: DVD 1 *VIDEO CLIPS for the Right-Handed Boxer*

AGAINST A LEFT-HANDED BOXER

1. Introduction
   a. Newton's Second Law of Motion
   b. Stance
   c. Boxing off your Back Foot
   d. Essential Footwork
   e. Footwork drills with 3 Angles
      1). The "Pivot"
      2). The "Step Around" (Step and Pivot)
      3). The "Bump" (Dip and Hop)

2. Offense –Practice throwing
   a. LEFT JAB
   b. The STRAIGHT RIGHT
   c. First Combination
   d. LEFT HOOK
      1) Short Range
      2) Long Range
   e. The Second Combination

3. Purpose of Ring Drills: To allow the beginner to improve skills in the ring without the risk of being injured or hurt, "to teach not injure".

4. Position goals for your feet and hands: Your **LEFT FOOT** should be outside opponent's right foot. Clockwise movement away from your opponent's power left hand. **OPEN YOUR RIGHT HAND**, and move your right glove to a position in front of your face (chin). Your left arm should be outside and higher than opponent's right hand.

5. Defense-Practice blocks/counter punches
   a. Blocks against RIGHT JAB - block open (palm) left hand.
   b. Blocks against STRAIGHT LEFT - block open (palm) right hand.
   c. Blocks against The First Combination - block open (palm) left hand and block open (palm) right hand
   d. Blocks against RIGHT HOOK - block with back of left hand
      1) Short Range
      2) Long Range
   e. Blocks against The Second Combination - all three blocks.
   f. Counter punches against RIGHT JAB - counter is a LEFT JAB.
   g. Counter punches against STRAIGHT LEFT - counter is a LEFT JAB.
   h. Counter punches against The First Combination - counter is a LEFT JAB.
   i. Counter punches against RIGHT HOOK - counter **depends** where your weight is distributed
      1) If your weight is on your **back foot**, turn ankles 90 degrees, counter punch is a STRAIGHT RIGHT.
      2) If your weight is on your **front foot**, counter punch is a LEFT HOOK.
   j. Counter punches against The Second Combination - counter depends where your weight is distributed:
      1) If your weight is on your **back foot**, counter punch is a STRAIGHT RIGHT.
      2) If your weight is on your **front foot,** counter punch is a LEFT HOOK.

6. Advanced footwork drills
   a. Cutting off the ring   b. Fighting off the ropes   c. Fighting out of a corner

Part 4: "Ring Drills" for the Right-Handed Boxer

Table 4-1: Novice RIGHT-Handed Boxer vs. Experienced RIGHT-Handed Boxer

Summary of Blocks and Counter Punches by a Novice RIGHT-Handed Boxer

	Punch From Right-Handed Boxer	Block By Novice Right-Handed Boxer	Counter Punch By Novice Right-Handed Boxer
A.	LEFT JAB	Open (palm) Right Hand	**LEFT JAB**
B.	STRAIGHT RIGHT	Left forearm, turning ankles clockwise 90°, place body weight on back foot	**STRAIGHT RIGHT**
C.	LEFT HOOK	Back Right Hand or back of right forearm	1. If weight on **back foot**, **STRAIGHT RIGHT**. 2. If weight on **front foot**, **LEFT HOOK**.

Table 4-2: Novice RIGHT-Handed Boxer vs. Experienced LEFT-Handed Boxer

Summary of Blocks and Counter Punches by a Novice RIGHT-Handed Boxer

	Punch From Left-Handed Boxer	Block By Novice Right-Handed Boxer	Counter Punch By Novice Right-Handed Boxer
A.	RIGHT JAB	Open (palm) Left Hand	**LEFT JAB**
B.	STRAIGHT RIGHT	Open (palm) Right Hand	**LEFT JAB**
C.	RIGHT HOOK	Back Left Hand or back of left forearm	1. If weight on **back foot**, **STRAIGHT RIGHT**. 2. If weight on **front foot**, **LEFT HOOK**.

PART 5: LESSONS FOR THE LEFT-HANDED BOXER

1. **Essential Human Anatomy for Boxers**

As a boxer, you must understand the location of some essential body parts such as the STERNUM (breastbone) located in the MIDDLE of the upper chest, the HEART located on the LEFT SIDE of the upper chest under the ribs. The LIVER is under the lower ribs on the RIGHT SIDE of the body. The "SOLAR PLEXUS" is located in the upper abdomen (stomach area) just below the rib cage. Punches landing in the area of the heart, liver or "solar plexus" can cause severe pain. The floating ribs, numbers 11 and 12, are not attached to the sternum. (Figure 1)

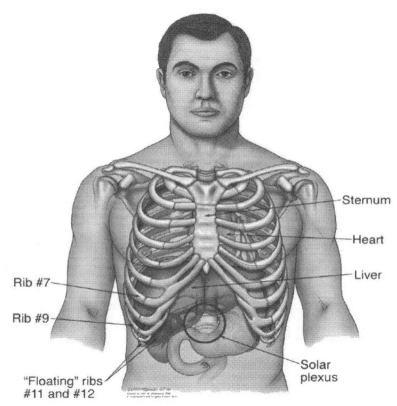

2. **Introduction VIDEO CLIPS**
a. **Newton's Second Law of Motion, Weight Transfer and a Forceful Punch**

A powerful punch is based on the science of physics and the laws of motion. Power punching requires understanding Newton's Second Law of Motion which is summarized and simplified by the formula F=MA. In the formula, F (force of your punch) is equal to your M (mass or your body weight) times A (acceleration or speed). Since your body weight is constant, to increase the force of your punch you must be able to accelerate (speed up) your movements. Therefore, a powerful, forceful punch comes from your ability to transfer your body weight rapidly combined with fast arm and fist motion. In other words, the ability to transfer your body weight from one place to another rapidly with a fast punching motion generates the forceful, powerful punch. The moment of impact is called: The Moment of Maximum Force (MMF).

Part 5: Lessons for the *Left-Handed Boxer*

b. Stance (Boxing Position, Fighting Position, Set Position or Set)
The Foundation of the Buffalo System

Your Stance is also called your Boxing Position or Fighting Position, Set Position, or just Set. You can use these terms interchangeably. The Stance is the starting point or foundation for "building a boxer." Learning and then knowing your own particular Stance or Set Position is the essential foundation, which must be INGRAINED into your body so it can be assumed almost as a reflex, at any moment. EVERYTHING you do, your footwork and your forceful, powerful punches begin with your Stance or Set Position. From this position, you are "Set" to move rapidly (explosively) with your footwork, thus you are "Set" on offense to move and punch forcefully with dynamic, explosive transfer of your entire body weight. You are also "Set" to defend yourself and counter punch when necessary.

c. Boxing off your Back Foot

Boxing off your back foot is essential to your ability to transfer your entire body weight (mass) from your back foot to your front foot, which allows you to produce a powerful, forceful punch with a STRAIGHT LEFT or a RIGHT HOOK transferring weight from front foot to back foot. It is that rapid transfer of your body weight (mass) that is essential to the Buffalo System of power punching. By boxing off the back foot you are also able to transfer or drive your weight (mass) forward WITHOUT transferring your weight from your back foot to your front foot when you throw the RIGHT JAB.

d. The RIGHT JAB

When throwing your RIGHT JAB, explosive motion of your right arm forward combined with explosive movement of your body weight (mass) forward generates the explosive, powerful punch and this is possible WITHOUT transferring your weight from your back foot to your front foot. By doing the lessons, you will learn how to throw a RIGHT JAB correctly and transfer or drive your weight (mass) forward WITHOUT transferring your weight from your back foot to your front foot when you throw the RIGHT JAB.

e. The STRAIGHT LEFT (Power Punch # 1)

Your first power punch is The STRAIGHT LEFT. The rapid (explosive) transfer of your body weight (mass) from the back foot to the front foot generates the power. In other words, it is the rapid (explosive) movement of your entire body forward from the back foot to the front foot that generates the tremendous force of your STRAIGHT LEFT punch. The point of maximum impact is termed MMF (Moment of Maximum Force). The faster you move your mass (your body weight) the greater the force of your punch! By throwing a STRAIGHT LEFT correctly, you transfer your entire body weight from your back foot to your front foot.

f. The RIGHT HOOK (Power Punch #2)

After throwing your STRAIGHT LEFT, your entire body weight transfers from your back foot to the front foot. With your body weight over your front foot, you can now throw a powerful RIGHT HOOK. The RIGHT HOOK, when thrown correctly, rapidly (explosively) transfers your entire body weight backwards from the front foot to the back foot.

In summary, fast (rapid and explosive) transfer of your body weight from one foot to the other is essential to generate a forceful punch. For a powerful STRAIGHT LEFT, you must rapidly transfer your body weight from your back foot to your front foot. For a powerful RIGHT HOOK, you must rapidly transfer your body weight from your front foot to your back foot. Therefore, a forceful, powerful punch requires the coordinated and balanced transfer of body weight. When throwing your RIGHT JAB, explosive motion of your right arm forward combined with explosive movement of your body weight (mass) forward generates the forceful, powerful punch and this possible WITHOUT transferring your weight from your back foot to your front foot. By mastering these lessons, you will learn how to throw the first three essential punches correctly with power.

g. Balance and awareness of your Body Weight Location

Successful development of boxing skills begins with the awareness of your Body Weight Location and its influence on your balance. You cannot box and punch effectively if you are off balance, and it is the awareness of your Body Weight Location that helps you understand balance. By doing the lessons, you will understand Body Weight Location, also called Body Weight Distribution and Balance.

All of the following lessons are building blocks, where each lesson progresses and builds upon the previous lesson. Study and master each lesson (building block) before progressing onto the next building block (lesson); otherwise, a flawed and imperfect boxer results. So, let's begin.

3. **Lesson 1: Balance and awareness of your Body Weight Location (Distribution)**
   Related to the position of your chin
   As a boxer, you must understand that a powerful, forceful punch comes from transferring every once of your total body weight with every punch thrown at a fast speed. You must be able to "transfer every ounce of your total body weight with every punch thrown"!

As a new boxer, the first essential you must fully understand is the location of your total body weight so you can learn how to quickly, rapidly and explosively transfer that full body weight with each of your first three essential punches. The position of your chin determines where your weight is distributed.

Understanding the location and distribution of your body weight is essential in order to quickly transfer your body weight effectively. To understand your body weight distribution, first straddle one of the lines painted on the floor. (5-1) When your chin is placed directly over your foot, it's impossible to lift your foot without moving your chin from over your foot because your entire body weight is over the foot making it impossible to lift that foot. (5-2)

5-1 When straddling a floor line, the distribution of your body weight is between your legs evenly distributed on both feet. You can't move either foot without moving your chin. The position of your chin determines the location of your body weight. Your CENTERLINE is an imaginary vertical line (vertical axis) starting at the top of your head extending down between your eyes and going further down between your legs.

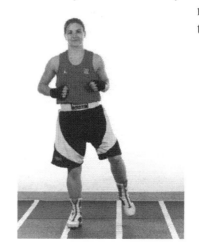

5-2 By lifting your left foot, moving your chin to the right of your CENTERLINE it is now impossible to lift your right foot.

Part 5: Lessons for the *Left-Handed Boxer*

The same holds true when you place your chin over your other foot. (53) You are unable to lift your foot without moving your chin. Your chin position (location) determines your Body Weight Location. Total awareness of the location and distribution of your body weight is the first step in building a boxer so that eventually you will be able to develop powerful, forceful punches by transferring every ounce of your total body weight with every punch you throw at very fast speeds.

5-3 By lifting your right foot, moving your chin left of your CENTERLINE it is now impossible to lift your left foot.

4. **Lesson 2: Stance (Boxing Position, Fighting Position, Set Position or Set)**

Once you understand the location and distribution of your body weight, the next essential is establishing your own individual Stance, Boxing Position, also called Fighting Position, Set Position or Set.

Set Position or Set for short, is the foundation or platform on which a boxer is built. (5-4) From Set Position, you can do almost EVERYTHING in boxing. You can move rapidly with your footwork and punch effectively on offense or block an opponent's punches on defense. Learning your own Set Position is essential since everything you do in boxing begins with your Stance (also called Boxing Position, Fighting Position, Set Position or just Set.)

a. Your Feet

Stand with your feet about shoulder width apart on each side of a floor line. The right foot is on the right side of the floor line and the left foot is on the left side of the line each at a 45-degree angle to the line. Raise the heel of your back foot off the ground so you can move quickly. Slightly bend your knees. (5-4)

b. Your Hands

Position the left hand with the thumb resting against the left side of your face (jaw–chin) protecting it. Your left forearm should be resting against your rib cage protecting the ribs. (5-4) The liver is on the other side, the right side under the ribs. The right hand is approximately 10 to 12 inches (2 fists) in front of the face just under the right eye. The thumb of both hands should be facing up. It is essential that your chin is "tucked in" below your shoulders. Your right shoulder points forward at your opponent's chest or your reflection in the mirror. Roll your upper back and shoulders to the left placing the chin in the left side of the line with the chin lining up just forward of the back or left foot. (5-4)

5-4 Your own individual Stance is also called Boxing Position, Fighting Position, Set Position or Set for the Left-Handed boxer. Note the position of the chin, hands, elbows, knees and feet with the body weight distributed over the back foot, behind your CENTERLINE. The heel of the back foot is off the floor.

c. Your Body Weight

Feel that your body weight is on the balls of your feet. The majority of your body weight must be distributed over the ball of the back foot, which is behind your CENTERLINE. Your CENTERLINE is an imaginary vertical line (vertical axis) starting at the top of your head extending down between your eyes and going further down between your legs, evenly distributing the weight over each foot. When your chin is behind your CENTERLINE your body weight is distributed or located over your back foot and conversely when your chin is in front of your CENTERLINE your body weight is distributed or located over your front foot. Now you have assumed your Stance or Fighting Position, Boxing Position,

Set Position or Set. (5-4) Check your Stance with your coach and in the mirror. From the essential Set Position, you can do almost everything in boxing You are set to move in any direction with your footwork and deliver your punches on offense or protect yourself on defense. When in your Stance be sure to feel that your body weight is behind your CENTERLINE with the majority of your body weight distributed or located over your back or rear foot in your Stance. This is exactly how you want to feel. Weight distributed behind your CENTERLINE over your back foot in your unique Stance. This is your Fighting Position, Boxing Position or Set Position. You **MUST** ask your coach to check your Stance **BEFORE** you continue with the next lesson.

5. Lesson 3: Balance and Loss of Balance

In boxing you always begin in your Stance, Boxing Position, Fighting Position, Set Position or Set. Your Stance is your foundation position. You must feel balanced in that Stance. (5-4) As the boxer moves the chin upwards, the body weight transfers to heels of the feet, the toes point upwards (arrows), the boxer is off balance and falls backwards. Of course, you must always AVOID losing your balance. (5-5)

6. Lesson 4: Essential Footwork—Learning to Box off your Back Foot

a. Movement Forward

Practice this lesson in front of a mirror using the floor lines. Always begin in Set Position. (5-6) Start at one end of the line and move toward the mirror. When you reach the mirror at the end of the line, just walk back to the starting line and begin again. Always begin in your Stance, your Boxing Position (Set Position). (5-6) Boxers move by opening their Stance and closing it. Learn to move out of Set Position and back into Set Position. Every second step will put you, the boxer,

5-5 Moving the chin up transfers the body weight to the heels of the feet, pointing the toes upward (arrows) as the boxer loses balance causing a backward fall.

back into Boxing Position (Set Position). Move forward by pushing or driving off the ball of the back foot moving the front foot forward (**about 6 inches**) "opening" or widening the Stance. (5-7) Then close the Stance by sliding the back foot forward re-assuming Boxing Position back into Set Position. (5-8) The boxer's front foot meets the floor toes first. **DO NOT** meet the floor heel first because this will put you in an unbalanced position. A boxer **ALWAYS** moves on the balls of the feet. The boxer's body weight MUST always be on the balls of the feet. The heel of the boxer's back foot remains approximately **ONE INCH OFF THE FLOOR** through the lesson.

5-6 Stance (Set Position) viewed from the side.

5-7 MOVING FORWARD by pushing off the ball of the back foot (driving open the Stance) and driving the front foot forward. (arrow)

5-8 Sliding the back foot forward (arrow) closing the Stance back into a new Set Position

Part 5: Lessons for the *Left-Handed Boxer*

In order to transfer your weight and punch with power, you MUST learn to move with your footwork while still maintaining your body weight (mass) over your back foot. While moving forward, the challenge is maintaining your body weight primarily over the back foot by keeping your chin over your back foot, rear or behind your own body CENTERLINE. Start this movement forward until you reach the end of a line about 30 feet (10 yards) away. Then walk back to the starting line and repeat moving forward still maintaining your body weight over the back foot, rear of your own body CENTERLINE.

The coach is present for this lesson, and once you can consistently open and close your Stance and consistently return to Boxing Position (Set Position) going forward maintaining your weight behind or rear of your CENTERLINE over your back foot, you are ready for the next lesson. Accomplishing this lesson and finally feeling natural and comfortable with your Boxing Position (Stance, Set Position) and your body weight distributed behind your CENTERLINE over your back foot may require several days of daily practice. **Again, you may require SEVERAL DAYS of daily practice to master this lesson but do not proceed to the next lesson until you master maintaining your body weight over your back foot behind (rear) of your CENTERLINE. Unless you master this lesson you will be a flawed boxer and unable to perform the essential explosive footwork movements and the power punching skills with sustained efficiency to become a champion. You must learn to move in all directions while maintaining your weight rear of your CENTERLINE. As a boxer you MUST have the ability to transfer your body weight (mass) with your JAB still maintaining your body weight rear of the CENTERLINE on your back foot. For your STRAIGHT LEFT you must be able to transfer your body weight through the CENTERLINE from your back foot to your front foot that is where your power of your STRAIGHT LEFT comes from, that transfer of your body weight through the CENTERLINE. Alternately to develop the power of your RIGHT HOOK you must be able to rapidly transfer your body weight from the front foot to the back foot again transferring your entire body weight from the front foot to the back foot through the CENTERLINE. This lesson must be MASTERED before progressing to the next lesson.**

b. Movement Backward

Perform this next lesson in front of the mirror with floor lines and always start in Boxing Position (Set Position). (5-9) Move backwards by pushing or driving off the ball of your front foot opening your Stance by pushing the back foot back **about 6 inches**. (5-10) Then slide the front foot back to Boxing Position (Set Position). (5-11) Your body weight MUST remain centered over the back foot at all times when moving forward and backward.

5-9 Start in Set Position

5-10 MOVING BACKWARD by pushing off the ball of the foot (driving open the Stance) and driving the back foot backward, (arrow)

5-11 Sliding the front foot backward (arrow) closing the Stance back into a new Set Position.

c. Movement to Left and Right

This lesson is done in front of the mirror with floor lines and always starts in Boxing Position (Set Position). (5-12) You **ALWAYS** push off the foot opposite to the direction you intend to move.

1) Moving to the Left

The boxer begins in Boxing Position (Set Position) driving open your stance. (5-12). The boxer moves to the LEFT by pushing off the RIGHT FOOT. (5-13) The boxer then slides the right foot back to Boxing Position (Set Position). (5-14) You always begin in Boxing Position then move in the desired direction and always return to Boxing Position (Set Position). You must always look exactly the same in your Boxing Position (Set Position) before starting a movement and after completing a movement.

5-12 Start in Set Position

5-13 **MOVING TO THE LEFT** (arrow) by pushing off the ball of the opposite (right) foot.

5-14 Sliding your right foot (arrow) to the left back into Set Position.

2) Moving to the Right

The boxer begins in Boxing Position (Set Position). (5-15) The boxer moves to the RIGHT by pushing off the LEFT FOOT driving open your stance. (5-16) The boxer then slides the left foot back to Boxing Position (Set Position). (5-17) Once you can consistently move forward, backward and laterally to both the right and left while consistently maintaining Boxing Position (Set Position) with the body weight positioned over your back foot, you are ready for the coach's drill.

5-15 Start in Set Position

5-16 MOVING TO THE RIGHT (arrow) by pushing off the ball of the opposite (left) foot.

5-17 Sliding your left foot (arrow) to the right back into Set Position.

Part 5: Lessons for the *Left-Handed Boxer*

The Coach's Drill

Have your coach stand in front of you and point in the direction you must move. You **MUST** be able t
change directions quickly on the balls of your feet keeping your body weight over your back foot. The toe
of your shoes must not leave the floor when you are in Boxing Position (Set Position). If the front of you
shoes or toes rises off the floor, you are off balance, and loss of balance must always be avoided.

7. **Lesson 5: Essential Footwork—"Step-and-a-Half"**

This lesson is done in front of the mirror with the floor lines and always starts in Boxing Position (Set
Position). (5-18) This lesson helps you understand rapid (explosive) footwork movement and range. A
boxer must **NEVER LUNGE** or take large steps. You must take small steps, moving explosively
(powerfully) from Boxing Position (Set Position) and back into Boxing Position (Set Position) while always
maintaining balance in your proper Stance with the body weight distributed over the back foot. The purpose
of "Step-and-a-Half" is to move rapidly (explosively) into a new position and closing range without lunging
(getting closer to an opponent) to punch effectively.

a. **Forward**

To accomplish "Step-and-a-Half" forward start in the Boxing Position (Set Position) (5-18), the boxer firs
steps forward (5-19) and hops forward (5-20) by pushing off the back foot and landing on the back foot firs
in Boxing Position (Set Position). (5-21) Once you are able to perform "Step-and-aHalf" consistentl
forward, you must also learn to go backward.

5-18 Start in Set

5-19 **"STEP-AND-A-HALF"
FORWARD** Stepping forward
first.

5-20 Then hopping forward
landing on the back foot.
(arrows)

5-21 Back into set position

b. Backward

Start in Boxing Position (Set Position). (5-22) Push off the front foot (5-23) and stepping with back foot and hopping (5-24) backwards landing on the front foot first into Boxing Position (Set Position). (5-25)

5-22 Start in Set Position.

5-23 **"STEP-AND-A-HALF" BACKWARD** Stepping backward first. (arrow)

5-24 Then hopping backward landing on the front foot first.

5-25 Back into Set Position.

c. To The Right

This lesson starts in Boxing Position (Set Position). (5-26) To take a "Step-and-a-Half" to the right, the boxer steps to the right by pushing off the left foot (5-27) and hops (5-28) to the right landing on the back foot first back into Boxing Position (Set Position). (5-29)

5-26 Start in Set Position.

5-27 **"STEP-AND-A-HALF" TO THE RIGHT** Stepping to the right first. (arrow)

5-28 Hopping to the right landing on the back foot first. (arrow)

5-29 Back into Set Position.

Part 5: Lessons for the *Left-Handed Boxer*

d. To The Left

The boxer starts in Boxing Position (Set Position). (5-30) To take a "Step-and-a-Half" to the left, the boxer steps to the left pushing off the right foot (5-31) opening the Stance to the left and hops (5-32) to left back landing on the front foot first into Set Position (Boxing Position). (5-33)

5-30 Start in Set Position.

5-31 **"STEP-AND-A-HALF" TO THE LEFT** Stepping to the left first. (arrow)

5-32 Hopping to the left landing on the front foot first, (arrows)

5-33 Back into Set Position.

8. Lesson 6: Essential Footwork--The "Pivot"

Perform this lesson in front of the mirror with floor lines and always start in Boxing Position (Set Position). (5-34) The "Pivot" is the first essential step to understanding angles. The boxer pivots or spins one quarter turn or 90 degrees counter-clockwise (rotating on the front right foot with your head and body turning to your Left) on the ball of the front foot while maintaining Boxing Position (Set Position). (5-35) Practice The "Pivot" counter-clockwise 90 degrees (rotating on your front right foot) turning 4 times until you are back to the beginning in Boxing Position (Set Position). Now pivot in the opposite direction by starting in Boxing Position (Set Position) and pivot (5-36) a quarter turn or 90 degrees clockwise (rotating on your front right foot toward the right with your head and body turning to your Right) on the ball of the front foot while maintaining Boxing Position (Set Position). (5-37) Next practice The "Pivot" clockwise 4 times until you are back to starting position. You must be able to pivot counter-clockwise (rotating to the left) and pivot clockwise (rotating to the right) before going on to the next lesson.

5-34 Start in Set Position.

5-35 **PIVOT COUNTER-CLOCKWISE** (turning to your to left) on the ball of your front (right) foot (arrow shows boxer facing new direction after a counter-clockwise pivot).

5-36 Start in Set Position.

5-37 **PIVOT CLOCKWISE** (turning to your right) on the ball of your front (right) foot (arrow shows boxer facing new direction after clockwise pivot.)

9. Lesson 7: Essential Footwork--The "Step Around" (Step and Pivot)

Perform this lesson in front of the mirror with floor lines and always start in Boxing Position (Set Position). (5-38) The "Step Around" is a small step to the right with the right foot (5-39) followed by a pivot counter-clockwise on the right foot(rotating to the left with your head and body TURNING to your LEFT). (5-40) The "Step Around" (Step and Pivot) to the right develops an angle to the opponent's left.

5-38 Start in Set Position.

5-39 Step to the right. (arrow)

5-40 "STEP AROUND" Pivot counter-clockwise (turning to the left) on the ball of your front (right) foot (arrow shows boxer facing a new direction after a counter-clockwise pivot). It is the Step with The "Pivot" that defines The "Step Around" which changes the angle 90 degrees.

10. Lesson 8: Essential Footwork--The "Scissor Step"

Perform this lesson in front of the mirror with floor lines and always start in Boxing Position (Set Position). (5-41) The "Scissor Step" is the quickest way for a Left-Handed Boxer to move laterally to the right. The boxer opens the Stance equally and in opposite directions (5-42) and then slides the left foot back to Boxing Position (Set Position). (5-43)

5-41 Start in Set Position.

5-42 "SCISSORS STEP" Opening the Stance equally in opposite directions (arrows going to the right and left at the same time.

5-43 Sliding the left foot (arrow) back into Set Position resulting in movement to the right.

Part 5: Lessons for the Left-Handed Boxer

11. Lesson 9: Rhythm

Rhythm is the flow or movement of rocking back and forth in Boxing Position (Set Position). You **MUST** ask your coach to check your Essential Footwork and Rhythm (Lesson 5-9) **BEFORE** you continue with the next lesson, the **RIGHT JAB.**

12. Lesson 10: The RIGHT JAB

Perform this lesson in front of the mirror with the floor lines and always start in Boxing Position (Set Position). The RIGHT JAB is the left handed boxer's most important punch. The Jab helps determine the distance or range to the opponent. By using the Jab, you can break or disrupt the opponent's rhythm. The RIGHT JAB prepares the boxer to throw the left hand power punch. The boxer assumes Boxing Position (Set Position) on the lines in front of the mirror. (5-44) As soon as you start to throw the RIGHT JAB, the right foot simultaneously steps forward and lands on the floor at exactly the same time as the right arm is fully extended. (5-45) Your upper torso turns and rolls to the left with the right shoulder resting against the right side of the jaw. The boxer must **EXHALE WHILE THROWING THE PUNCH.** As soon as the right arm is fully extended with the wrist turned over, the right arm retracts in a straight line back to Boxing Position (Set Position) as the left (back) foot moves forward. (5-46) The punch mechanics of the RIGHT JAB begins as the boxer throws the RIGHT JAB in a straight line from Boxing Position (Set

5-44 Start in Set Position for the RIGHT JAB.

5-45 **RIGHT JAB** Exactly as the FRONT foot moves forward (arrow), the punching right arm moves forward. The right arm is fully extended as the right foot hits the floor. The upper body (torso) rolls to the left as the right shoulder rolls against the right side of the face (protecting the jaw-chin).

5-46 **RIGHT JAB** Exactly as the BACK foot slides forward, the punching right arm moves backward into Set Position.

Position) while turning the wrist and hand over so the boxer's knuckles are parallel to the floor with the wrist fixed in a straight line. (5-47a and b) (5-48 and 5-49) The footwork for the Jab and associated weight transfer is such that as the boxer initiates the RIGHT JAB, the right front foot moves forward opening the Stance, and as the wrist and hand turn over and as the arm is fully extended, the right front foot lands on the floor at the exact same time as the body weight transfers forward pushing off the back leg. The boxer's chin must remain behind the CENTERLINE or vertical axis **STILL KEEPING THE BODY WEIGHT ON THE BACK LEFT FOOT**. The back leg and boxer's right arm return to Boxing Position (Set Position) at the same time. The Jab is most effective when the arm is fully extended as the front foot hits the floor with a small step at range so that the punch lands on the opponent with the arm fully extended. The Jab is similar to the stinging produced by snapping a towel. The sting from snapping a towel is most effective when the towel is fully extended. The snapping towel is less effective at producing a sting when the range is shortened and the towel is too close to the subject. The same is true of the Jab. The Jab is most effective when it hits your opponent with your arm fully extended as your body weight and momentum transfers forward. The boxer should target the Jab to the opponent's eye since a Jab in the eye will obscure vision and can tilt the opponent's head back. By tilting the opponent's head backward, the chin moves upward, causing the opponent's body weight to transfer backward with the opponent losing balance. In addition with the head tilting backward, the opponent's chin is vulnerable to your power punch, the STRAIGHT LEFT hand which can be thrown as your next punch. You **MUST** ask your coach to check your Right Jab **BEFORE** you continue with the next lesson.

5-47b

5-49

5-47 a

5-48

5-47 a and b **RIGHT JAB** With the boxer facing you, notice the turning of the wrist (5-48) and hand so the boxer's knuckles rotate to become parallel to the floor at the end of the punch (5-49) and the right shoulder protects the right side of the face (jaw-chin).

13. **Lesson 11: Practicing Range**

First practice the RIGHT JAB in front of the mirror, and when the mechanics of the punch are mastered, and checked by the coach you then practice the RIGHT JAB on the heavy bag by starting in Boxing Position (Set Position). First touch the heavy bag with a fully extended right hand on the bag **WITHOUT** taking a step. (5-50) Then step back a half step (**about 6 inches**) with the back left foot and then with the front right foot back into Boxing Position (Set Position). (5-51) Now take a small step (about 6 inches) forward to hit the bag. (5-52) This is the boxer's RANGE. This is your range. Practice the Jab on the heavy bag by hitting the bag in the middle of the swing as it comes toward you. You should time the punch so the Jab hits the bag with the arm fully extended ("locked out") while taking a small step forward. You are too close to the bag if, as the bag is hit, the bag is pushed forward causing the bag to swing. The bag will make a popping sound when it is hit at the correct range causing the bag to stop swinging. The boxer's head should **NEVER** be directly in front of the bag when the Jab strikes the bag. With a correctly thrown RIGHT JAB, your head and upper torso must roll to your left with the right shoulder rolling against the jaw, protecting the jaw, placing the head slightly to the left of the bag. Now the boxer will start to understand range.

Timing is correct when striking the bag with the RIGHT JAB at the center of its swing (causing the bag to stop) and as the right foot hits the floor. The range is correct when the bag is struck with the RIGHT JAB after taking a small step with the right arm fully extended or "locked out". The boxer must time the landing of the punch as the front right foot hits the floor. Every punch should set up another punch. The RIGHT JAB sets up the STRAIGHT LEFT. The RIGHT JAB must be practiced in front of the mirror and on the heavy bag until all aspects of the mechanics and breathing are mastered, remembering to **EXHALE** while throwing each punch. Once range is understood and reproduced in front of your coach, you may then "dance" with the bag and practice your RIGHT JAB with a moving heavy bag. You **MUST** ask your coach to check your Range **BEFORE** you continue with the next lesson.

5-50 Practicing the RIGHT JAB on the heavy bag first by touching the bag with the right hand in Set Position.

5-51 Next with both feet take a small step (about 6 inches) back (arrow) away from the bag with both the front and back feet returning to Set Position.

5-52 Right Jab Taking a small step (about 6 inches) forward to hit the bag. This is the boxer's range. Strike the bag as it swings back toward you. Hit the bag in the middle of the swing. When hit correctly, a popping sound occurs as the bag stops swinging.

14. Lesson 12: Dancing with the bag (reinforcing footwork) at range

The coach pushes the heavy bag so it swings forward and backward in a straight line. The boxer is told to move back and forth keeping the bag at range with the essential footwork already learned. Use your footwork keeping the heavy bag in range at all times so you can take that small step striking the heavy bag with your fully extended RIGHT JAB. Next, the coach pushes the heavy bag side to side, and the boxer moves laterally to the right and left keeping the bag at range. The coach next pushes the bag in different directions with the boxer using the essential footwork maintaining Boxing Position (Set Position) in front of the heavy bag at range and striking the bag with the RIGHT JAB on command by the coach. After this is mastered, you can work with the heavy bag on your own, pushing the heavy bag in different directions and staying in range striking the bag with the RIGHT JAB, remembering to **EXHALE** while throwing the RIGHT JAB.

15. Lesson 13: Dancing with the bag--The "Pivot" (The First Angle) at range

Now the boxer learns to keep the bag at range using The "Pivot" (The First Angle). The boxer hits the bag with the RIGHT JAB and then pivots. The boxer must practice The Jab and Pivot while returning to Boxing Position (Set Position) in front of the heavy bag at range. As the coach changes the bag's direction, the boxer moves on the balls of the feet, opening and closing Boxing Position (Set Position) returning to Boxing Position with every second step. The coach must observe and always correct the boxer's footwork to be sure the footwork is performed correctly. Practice The "Pivot" staying in range so you can hit the swinging bag with your RIGHT JAB.

16. Lesson 14: Dancing with the bag--The "Step Around" (Step and Pivot) (The Second Angle) at range

The coach pushes the heavy bag, and when the bag reaches the center of its swing, the boxer throws the RIGHT JAB then takes a first step to the right and pivots to be in position to hit the bag again with a fully extended RIGHT JAB. Practice the "Step Around" (Step and Pivot) to the right staying in range so you can hit the swinging bag with your RIGHT JAB.

17. Lesson 15: Dancing with the bag--The "Scissor Step" at range

The boxer practices the "Scissors Step" to the right to be in position to hit the bag with a fully extended RIGHT JAB at range.

18. Lesson 16: The STRAIGHT LEFT (Power Punch One)

Standing in front of the mirror with the floor lines starting in Boxing Position (Set Position), the STRAIGHT LEFT is a power or "knockout" punch. In order to throw this punch correctly, you must be able to transfer your body weight from the back foot to the front foot. The boxer starts in Boxing Position (Set Position). (5-53) The boxer will transfer body weight from the back foot to the front foot by turning (pivoting) on the toe (ball) of the left foot, moving the heel to the left or clockwise as the boxer's body weight transfers from the back foot to the front foot. (5-54) Note: As the chin passes through the boxer's CENTERLINE to the front foot, this movement forces the shoulders and hips to "square up." (5-55) The boxer's feet will be spaced the same distance apart as they were in Boxing Position (Set Position). The boxer's knee over the front leg will bend slightly as the back foot pivots, placing the chin directly over the front knee and over the toe of the front foot. (5-56) This is called the **"3-Point Line-Up"**:

1) **The point of the chin**
2) **The point of the knee**
3) **The point of the toe**

Therefore, the chin, and knee are lined up directly over the toe of the front foot. By bending the knee ("sitting down on the punch"), the boxer transfers the body weight to the ball of the front foot while maintaining balance. Before the punch is thrown, the boxer's head and chin are positioned rear of the CENTERLINE and just in front of the back (left) foot with the body weight over the back (left) foot. After the punch is thrown, the chin and the body weight is transferred over the front (right) foot. When the boxer finishes bending the knee or "sitting down on the punch", the body weight drops straight down toward the floor. "Sitting down on the punch" allows a boxer to control his or her own inertia. By dropping the body weight straight down toward the floor, the boxer's balance is maintained as the body weight transfers from the back foot to the front foot, keeping the boxer from falling forward and losing balance.

5-53 Start in Set Position for the **STRAIGHT LEFT**.

5-54 **STRAIGHT LEFT** The boxer transfers the body weight from the back foot to the front foot as the chin moves through the CENTERLINE and the "3-Point Line-Up" is achieved. The 3 points (from top to bottom) are: 1) the chin, 2) the front (right) knee and 3) the toe of the front (right) foot.

5-55 As the **STRAIGHT LEFT** is thrown, with the weight transfer from the back foot to the front foot, passes through the CENTERLINE and the hips and shoulders are "squared up", (hips and shoulders facing directly forward). The heal of the left foot is elevated with the **STRAIGHT LEFT**.

5-56 Note the "3-Point Line-Up" of the chin, right knee and the right toe.

Part 5: Lessons for the *Left-Handed Boxer*

The STRAIGHT LEFT starts on the left side of the boxer's chin with the elbow resting against the rib cage. The left elbow and the left hip rotate or turn through the punch together. The left arm should lie against the boxer's rib cage all the way through the punch. The left shoulder should come to rest against the left side of the boxer's face, protecting the boxer from a counter punch while protecting the jaw. The fast twitch muscles used to throw this punch are primarily the anterior deltoid muscles (one of the muscles that form the rounded contour of the shoulder). The STRAIGHT LEFT should be aimed at your opponent's chin. You must EXHALE as the punch is thrown and retract your arm as quickly as possible back into Boxing Position (Set Position). You MUST ask your coach to check your Straight Left BEFORE you continue with the next lesson.

19. Lesson 17: The First Combination—Two Punches (RIGHT JAB and a STRAIGHT LEFT)

Each punch (when thrown correctly) will "set up" or prepare you to throw another punch. The RIGHT JAB "sets up" the STRAIGHT LEFT. The First Combination every left-handed boxer learns is the RIGHT JABAB followed by a STRAIGHT LEFT. You always start in Boxing Position (Set Position). (5-57) The boxer opens the Stance with the RIGHT JAB fully extended to determine range. (5-58) The boxer then closes the Stance while moving (pivoting) the left foot clockwise "pushing" the ball of the left foot forward which simulates "squeezing" or "squishing" a bug into the floor. (5-59) The boxer's feet should be at a correct distance apart, approximating Set Position, maintaining balance after bringing the left foot forward. If the front foot moves forward 3 inches, the back foot comes forward 3 inches returning the boxer to Boxing Position (Set Position). When throwing the RIGHT JAB, your right shoulder will rest against the right side of your face while your torso rolls to the left. Now when throwing the STRAIGHT LEFT, your left shoulder will rest against the left side of your face while your body rolls to the right with the chin stopping directly over the right knee, which must line-up directly over the right front foot in the right front foot in the "3 Point Line-Up".

-57 Start in Set Position or the FIRST COMBINATION (RIGHT AB followed by the TRAIGHT LEFT).

5-58 Step forward (arrow) throwing the RIGHT JAB

5-59 The **STRAIGHT LEFT**, note the left shoulder protecting the jaw on the left side and "3Point Line-Up" with the chin, the right knee and the toe of the right foot in a straight line. The left foot has moved slightly forward, and rotated clockwise, pointing the toes forward as the left arm and hand are extended rapidly at exactly the same time as the weight transfers from the back foot (heel elevated) to the front foot, reaching the Moment of Maximum Force (MMF) for that punch. The faster the weight is transferred from the back foot to the front foot the greater the force of the punch, obeying Newton's Second Law (F=MA) where the force of the punch (F) is increased by the weight (M or mass) transfer multiplied by the speed of the punch (A or acceleration or simplified as speed of the punch). The **STRAIGHT LEFT**--Note that the "3-Point Line-Up" of the chin, right knee and toe of the right foot are in a straight line, with the body weight transferred from the rear foot to the front foot. Both feet are pointing forward with the heel of the back foot elevated.

Part 5: Lessons for the *Left-Handed Boxer*

The RIGHT JAB should be aimed at the opponent's eye obstructing vision and causing the opponent's chin to move up and back, redistributing the opponent's weight to the heels of the feet throwing the opponent off balance. The STRAIGHT LEFT should be aimed at the opponent's chin for the "knockout"!

A boxer must <u>NEVER</u> move straight back after throwing a STRAIGHT LEFT. A boxer moving straight back is vulnerable to being hit by either of the opponent's hands. The "Bump" (Dip and Hop) to the left is used after the STRAIGHT LEFT is thrown. The "Bump" is used to establish an angle (or "break" an angle) out of your opponent's range but still in your range. The "Bump" (Dip and Hop) to the left after throwing a STRAIGHT LEFT places your body weight on your back foot. The left leg must land on the floor directly under you as the floor stops your inertia. This allows you to avoid your opponent's offense by being out of the opponent's range yet you are in position to throw another left hand punch.

For the Left-Handed Boxer, the "Bump" is NOT an optimal angle since this moves the Left-Handed Boxer clockwise into the opponent's right hand. Our boxer must keep the hands high to block the opponent's potential right hand, and the "dip" movement often allows the boxer to slip underneath the opponent's STRAIGHT RIGHT. If on the other hand after the STRAIGHT LEFT, the Left-Handed Boxer ends up positioned outside of the opponent's left shoulder, the Left-Handed Boxer would prefer to "Step Around" (Step and Pivot) to the right. This allows the Left-Handed Boxer to avoid the opponent's offense by being out of the opponent's range yet the Left-Handed Boxer is in position to throw either a STRAIGHT LEFT or RIGHT JAB. You **MUST** ask your coach to check your First Combination **BEFORE** you continue with the next lesson.

20. Lesson 18: Practicing The First Combination (RIGHT JAB, STRAIGHT LEFT) on the Heavy Bag

Hit the heavy bag at range with a RIGHT JAB as you step and your head rolls to the left outside the bag. You head should NEVER stop directly in front of the bag. Next, you should immediately throw the STRAIGHT LEFT closing the stance back into Boxing Position (Set Position) as the head rolls to the right outside the bag. You **MUST** ask your coach to check your First Combination **BEFORE** you continue with the next lesson.

21. Lesson 19: The "Step Around" (Step and Pivot) to the right (The Second Angle) and The "Bump" (Dip and Hop) to the left (The Third Angle)

You must NEVER step straight back after throwing a STRAIGHT LEFT hand; therefore, after throwing the RIGHT JAB and STRAIGHT LEFT combination, you can either "Bump" to the left or "Step Around" to the right. In either situation, you move back into Boxing Position (Set Position), and you are in position to punch again with another STRAIGHT LEFT or another RIGHT JAB without being punched.

The First Angle is the "Pivot". The Second Angle is the "Step Around" (Step and Pivot) to the right. The Third Angle is the "Bump" (Dip and Hop) to the left. Developing angles allows you to be in an offensive position, to hit without being hit, outside your opponent's right and left hands placing the opponent in a defensive position. The "Step Around" to your right renders the opponent's right and left hands useless and the "Bump" to your left renders the opponent's left and right hands useless too. If after throwing a punch you end up positioned outside the opponent's left shoulder, the best angle is the "Step Around" (Step and Pivot) to the right. On the other hand, if you are positioned outside the opponent's right hand, the best angle is the "Bump" (Dip and Hop) to the left placing the opponent in a defensive position. Even though you are closer to the opponent's right hand, putting you in position to use the STRAIGHT LEFT while the opponent is out of position finding it difficult to throw the right hand effectively. Therefore, caution is advised as it is usually best for the Left-Handed Boxer to move counter-clockwise away from the opponent's power right hand; thus, after the STRAIGHT LEFT the boxer prefers the "Step Around" (The Second Angle) counter-clockwise and away from the opponent's power right hand.

22. Lesson 20: The RIGHT HOOK (Power Punch Two), (Short Range)

a. Footwork in Front of Mirror

The STRAIGHT LEFT sets up the RIGHT HOOK. The STRAIGHT LEFT ends with all of the boxer's weight on the ball of the front foot with the chin and knee lined up directly over the toes of the front foot in the "3-Point Line-Up". (5-60) The RIGHT HOOK starts as the boxer rapidly turns both ankles counter-clockwise (facing to the left) 90 degrees with the heel of his front foot off the ground and both knees slightly bent. This rapid turning of both feet transfers the entire body weight from the front foot to the back foot. The boxer's chin and left knee will now be directly over the toes of the left foot in the "3-Point Line-Up". The boxer must keep the shoulders rounded with the chin tucked below and against the right shoulder for defense and balance. (5-61)

5-60 The **STRAIGHT LEFT** sets up The **RIGHT HOOK** since the STRAIGHT LEFT ends with all the weight on the front right foot in the "3-Point Line-Up".

5-61 Note the right shoulder protecting the jaw on the right side and "3-Point Line-Up" with the chin, the left knee and the toe of the left foot in a straight line. The left foot and the right foot have both rotated counter-clockwise pointing the toes 90 degrees to the left as the right arm and hand are extended rapidly at exactly the same time as the weight transfers from the front foot (heel elevated) to the back foot reaching the Moment of Maximum Force (MMF) for that punch. The faster the weight is transferred from the front foot to the back foot, the greater the force of the punch obeying Newton's Second Law (F=MA) where the force of the punch F is increased by weight (M or mass) transfer (front foot to back foot) multiplied by the speed of the punch (A or acceleration or simplified as speed of the punch). Note also the heel of the front right foot is elevated with the RIGHT HOOK, and the heel of the left foot is elevated with the STRAIGHT LEFT.

b. Punch Mechanics Short Range RIGHT HOOK/Thumb pointing toward your face

The **RIGHT HOOK** can be thrown at different distances or ranges. The Short Range **RIGHT HOOK** is delivered across the boxer's body with the right arm bent 90 degrees and parallel to the floor. (5-62) (5-63) The boxer's right shoulder will rest against the chin providing defense. The Boxer's right thumb pointed toward their face. The MMF (Moment of Maximum Force) is generated at the end of the punch as it lands on the target and occurs just as the boxer transfers the entire body weight from the front foot to the back foot. You **MUST** ask your coach to check your Short Range **RIGHT HOOK BEFORE** you continue with the next lesson.

5-62 Side view of the Short Range RIGHT HOOK: Note this Short Range RIGHT HOOK with the right shoulder protecting the right side of the face (jaw-chin) and the right arm and right forearm at right angles to each other. The thumb of the right hand is pointing toward the boxer's face.

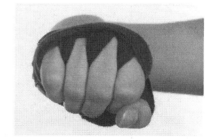

5-63 **SHORT RANGE RIGHT HOOK** Close-up of the right hand with the thumb facing the boxer's face.

Part 5: Lessons for the Left-Handed Boxer

23. Lesson 21: RIGHT HOOK (Power Punch Two), (Long Range)

a. Footwork in Front of Mirror

The foot work for the Long Range RIGHT HOOK is exactly the same as the foot work for the Short Range RIGHT HOOK with the transfer of body weight from the front foot to the back foot.

b. Punch Mechanics: Long Range RIGHT HOOK/Thumb pointing upward

Changing a **Short Range RIGHT HOOK** to a **Long Range RIGHT HOOK** requires extending your right arm by rotating your wrist away from your face thereby changing the position of the thumb from pointing towards your face to the "thumbs up" position. As the RIGHT HOOK extends past 90 degrees, you start to "ratchet" or rotate the wrist away from your face or clockwise causing the thumb to point further away from your face. A Long Range RIGHT HOOK lands with the thumb pointing upwards. (5-64) (5-65) Now it is **ESSENTIAL** that you begin practicing and eventually **MASTERING** all three punches and combinations on the heavy bag. You **MUST** ask your coach to check your Long Range RIGHT HOOK **BEFORE** you continue with the next lesson.

5-64 Side view of the **LONG RANGE RIGHT HOOK:** Note the Long Range RIGHT HOOK with the right shoulder protecting the right side of the face (jaw-chin) and the right arm and right forearm projecting further out away from the body. The right arm is at an angle that is greater than a right angle to the rib cage. The thumb of the right hand is beginning to rotate away from the boxer's face.

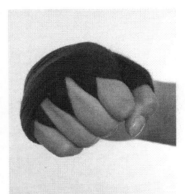

5-65 LONG RANGE RIGHT HOOK Close-up of the right hand with the thumb starting to rotate away from the boxer's face to a more "thumbs up" position.

24. Lesson 22- The Second Combination—Three Punches (RIGHT JAB, STRAIGHT LEFT, Short and Long Range RIGHT HOOK

a. Short Range

This Second Combination with the Short Range RIGHT HOOK must also be practiced and mastered on the heavy bag. Set Position (5-66), RIGHT JAB (5-67), STRAIGHT LEFT (5-68)

5-66 Start in Set Position for the **SECOND COMBINATION** (RIGHT JAB) followed by the STRAIGHT LEFT followed by the **SHORT RANGE RIGHT HOOK).**

5-67 **RIGHT JAB**

5-68 **STRAIGHT LEFT**

Short Range RIGHT HOOK. (5-69a & b)

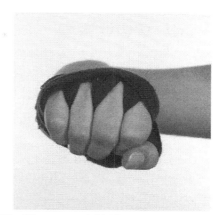

5-69a **SHORT RANGE RIGHT HOOK** Front view and note thumb pointing towards boxer's face.

5-69b Close up of **SHORT RANGE RIGHT HOOK** with thumb pointing towards boxer's face.

b. Long Range

This combination with the Long Range RIGHT HOOK must also be practiced and mastered on the heavy bag. Set Position (5-70), RIGHT JAB (5-71), STRAIGHT LEFT (3-72), Long Range LEFT HOOK, (5-73) Side view Long Range RIGHT HOOK, (5-74 You MUST ask your coach to check your Second Combination with both your Short Range and Long Range RIGHT HOOK BEFORE you continue with the next lesson.

-70 Start in Set Position for the **SECOND COMBINATION** (**RIGHT JAB**) followed by the **LONG RANGE RIGHT HOOK**).

5-71 **RIGHT JAB**

5-72 **STRAIGHT LEFT**

5-73 **LONG RANGE RIGHT HOOK**

5-74-Close up of the LONG RANGE RIGHT HOOK. Note the "thumb's up" position.

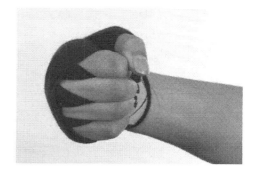

Part 5: Lessons for the *Left-Handed Boxer*

25. Lesson 23: Footwork with Angles

REMEMBER, NEVER finish a combination by moving straight back. It is essential to finish all your combinations by moving into a new position by developing angles (also termed "breaking an angle") so you can strike (punch) again without being hit. Therefore, it is essential that after any combination you move into a new position by developing an angle or "breaking an angle".

You must practice all three angles when working the heavy bag.
1. The First Angle is The "Pivot".
2. The Second Angle is The "Step Around" (Step and Pivot) to the **right**.
3. The Third Angle is The "Bump" (Dip and Hop) to the **left**.

Choosing the angle depends upon the position you are in after throwing the combination, and you may choose to use or develop any one of the three angles. For the Left-Handed Boxer after throwing a STRAIGHT LEFT the best is the Second Angle, the "Step Around" (Step and Pivot) to your right away for the Right-Handed opponent's power right hand. Developing angles allows you to be in an offensive position outside the opponent's right hand placing the opponent in a defensive position. The Third Angle, the "Bump" puts the opponent's both hands out of position, although the "Step Around" is usually the best angle for the Left Handed Boxer and renders the opponents right and left hands useless.

After throwing the STRAIGHT LEFT, you are in position to throw the RIGHT HOOK because all of your weight is on the ball of the front foot. Remember, to throw the RIGHT HOOK, you turn both ankles to the left (counter-clockwise) 90 degrees on the balls of the feet with the heel of the right (front) foot off the ground. Both knees should be slightly bent. This rapid movement will transfer all of your body weight to the back left (rear) foot. Your chin, left knee and the toes of the left foot will "line up" over each other in the "3-Point Line-Up".

It is essential that your shoulders be rounded with your chin tucked below against the right shoulder for defense and balance. As the Short Range RIGHT HOOK is thrown, your right arm comes across your body with the right arm bent 90 degrees and parallel to the floor. The thumb of your right hand will be pointed toward your face with the knuckles in a straight line parallel to the floor. Your chin will rest against your right shoulder providing defense. Since the MMF (Moment of Maximum Force) of your RIGHT HOOK occurs at the end of the punch, the punch should land on target just as your body weight transfers from the right (front) foot to the left (back) foot.

The RIGHT HOOK can be thrown at various distances or ranges. The Short Range RIGHT HOOK is thrown at a right angle or 90 degrees. To throw a longer range RIGHT HOOK start to rotate your right wrist and fist away from your face, causing the thumb of your right hand to point further away from the face extending the reach of the RIGHT HOOK. Now you **MUST** have your coach check all your punches, combinations, footwork and angles on the heavy bag so you can begin practicing and **MASTERING** these ESSENTIAL BOXING SKILLS **BEFORE** you do "Ring Drills" and

Part 6: DVD 2 🅳🆅🅳 *VIDEO CLIPS for the Novice Left-Handed Boxer*

PART 6:

A. FUNDAMENTALS
B. "RING DRILLS" AND SPARRING

This part covers the Fundamentals and "Ring Drills" including introduction to sparring for the beginner (novice) Left-Handed Boxer. The novice will learn to perform these "Ring Drills" against both a Right-Handed Boxer and a Left-Handed Boxer on both offense and defense learning the following in detail. It will all be covered on the DVD (video clips) in detail on DVD 2. Be sure to study the summary of Blocks and Counter Punches on Tables 6-1 and 6-2, page 90.

YOU WILL LEARN:

- How to throw the first 3 punches.
- How to throw the first 2 combinations.
- How to develop the essential 3 angles.
- How to defend against the first 3 punches.
- How to throw counter punches **AGAINST** a Right-Handed opponent.
- How to throw counter punches **AGAINST** a Left-Handed opponent.
- How to cut off the ring.
- How to fight off the ropes.
- How to fight out of a corner.

Part 6: DVD 2 💿 *VIDEO CLIPS for the Novice Left-Handed Boxer*
AGAINST A RIGHT-HANDED BOXER

1. Introduction
   a. Newton's Second Law of Motion
   b. Stance
   c. Boxing off your Back Foot
   d. Essential Footwork
   e. Footwork drills with 3 Angles
      1) The "Pivot"
      2) The "Step Around" (Step and Pivot)
      3) The "Bump" (Dip and Hop)

2. Offense – Practice throwing
   a. RIGHT JAB
   b. STRAIGHT LEFT
   c. The First Combination
   d. RIGHT HOOK
      1) Short Range
      2) Long Range
   e. The Second Combination

3. Purpose of "Ring Drills": To allow the beginner to improve skills in the ring without the risk of being injured or hurt, to "teach not injure".

4. Position goals for your feet and hands: Your **RIGHT FOOT** should be outside the opponent's left foot. Movement is counter-clockwise away from opponent's power hand. **OPEN YOUR LEFT HAND** and move your left glove to a position in front of your face (chin). Right hand should be outside and higher than opponent's left hand.

5. Defense – Practice blocks/counter punches after reading below about each block and each counter punch separately, DVD TWO shows the blocks and counter punches together.
   a. Blocks against LEFT JAB - block open (palm) right hand.
   b. Blocks against STRAIGHT RIGHT- block or catch with open left hand in front of chin.
   c. Blocks against The First Combination - block with open (palm) right hand and block or catch with open left hand in front of chin.
   d. Blocks against LEFT HOOK - block with back of right hand block.
   e. Blocks against The Second Combination - all three blocks.
   f. Counter punches against LEFT JAB - counter is a RIGHT JAB.
   g. Counter punches against STRAIGHT RIGHT- counter is a RIGHT JAB.
   h. Counter punches against The First Combination - counter is a RIGHT JAB.
   i. Counter punches against LEFT HOOK -counter **depends** where your weight is distributed:
      1) If your weight is on your **back foot**, turn ankles 90 degrees, counter punch is a STRAIGHT LEFT.
      2) If your weight is on your **front foot**, counter punch is a RIGHT HOOK.
   j. Counter punches against The Second Combination - counter depends on where your weight is distributed:
      1) If your weight is on your **back foot**, turn ankles 90 degrees - counter punch is a STRAIGHT LEFT.
      2) If your weight is on your **front foot** - counter punch is a RIGHT HOOK.

6. Advanced footwork drills
   a. Cutting off the ring
   b. Fighting off the ropes
   c. Fighting out of a corner

Part 6: DVD 2 💿 *VIDEO CLIPS for the Novice Left-Handed Boxer*
AGAINST A LEFT-HANDED BOXER

1. Introduction
   a. Newton's Second Law of Motion
   b. Stance
   c. Boxing off your Back Foot
   d. Essential Footwork
   e. Footwork drills with 3 Angles
      1) The "Pivot"
      2). The "Step Around" (Step and Pivot)
      3). The "Bump" (Dip and Hop)
2. Offense – Practice by throwing
   a. RIGHT JAB
   b. STRAIGHT LEFT
   c. The First Combination
   d. RIGHT HOOK
      1) Short Range
      2) Long Range
   e. The Second Combination
3. Purpose of "Ring Drills": To allow the beginner to improve skills in the ring without the risk of being injured or hurt, to "teach not injure"
4. Position goals for your feet: Your RIGHT SHOULDER should be facing your opponent's chest, and keep your opponent in front of you. Move either clockwise or counter-clockwise, always maintaining your opponent directly in front of you.
5. Defense – Practice blocks/counter punches
   a. Blocks against RIGHT JAB - open (palm) left hand block.
   b. Blocks against STRAIGHT LEFT - right forearm block and turn ankles 90 degrees counter-clockwise.
   c. Blocks against The First Combination - open (palm) left hand block and right forearm block and turn ankles 90 degrees counter-clockwise.
   d. Blocks against RIGHT HOOK - block with back of left hand
      1) Short Range
      2) Long Range
   e. Blocks against The Second Combination - all three blocks.
   f. Counter punches against RIGHT JAB - counter is a RIGHT JAB.
   g. Counter punches against STRAIGHT LEFT - counter is a STRAIGHT LEFT.
   h. Counter punches against The First Combination - counter is a STRAIGHT LEFT.
   i. Counter punches against RIGHT HOOK - counter **depends** where your weight is distributed:
      1) If your weight is on your **back foot** turn ankles 90 degrees, counter punch is a STRAIGHT LEFT.
      2) If your weight is on your **front foot**, counter punch is a RIGHT HOOK.
   j. Counter punches against The Second Combination – counter depends on where your weight is distributed:
      1) If your weight is on your back foot turn ankles 90 degrees - counter punch is a STRAIGHT LEFT.
      2) If your weight is on your front foot - counter punch is a RIGHT HOOK.
6. Advanced footwork drills
   a. Cutting off the ring
   b. Fighting off the ropes
   c. Fighting out of a corner

Part 6: "Ring Drills" for the Novice Left-Handed Boxer

Table 6-1: Novice LEFT-Handed Boxer vs. Experienced RIGHT-Handed Boxer

Summary of Blocks and Counter Punches by a Novice LEFT-Handed Boxer

	Punch From Right-Handed Boxer	Block By Novice Left-Handed Boxer	Counter Punch By Novice Left-Handed Boxer
A.	LEFT JAB	Open (palm) right hand	RIGHT JAB
B.	STRAIGHT RIGHT	Open (palm) left hand	RIGHT JAB
C.	LEFT HOOK	Back of right hand	1. If weight on **back foot**, **STRAIGHT LEFT.** 2. If weight on **front foot**, **RIGHT HOOK.**

Table 6-2: Novice LEFT-Handed Boxer vs. LEFT-Handed Boxer

Summary of Blocks and Counter Punches by a Novice LEFT-Handed Boxer

	Punch From Left-Handed Boxer	Block By Novice Left-Handed Boxer	Counter Punch By Novice Left-Handed Boxer
A.	RIGHT JAB	Open (palm) left hand	RIGHT JAB
B.	STRAIGHT LEFT	Right forearm, turning ankles counter-clockwise, placing body weight on back foot.	STRAIGHT LEFT
C.	RIGHT HOOK	Back of left hand	1. If weight on **back foot**, **STRAIGHT LEFT.** 2. If weight on **front foot**, **RIGHT HOOK.**

PART 7: ESSENTIAL RULES FOR "RING DRILLS" AND SPARRING

1. **Rules at the University at Buffalo Boxing Club**

   Before you begin the "Ring Drills" and sparring sessions, there are essential rules you MUST understand and follow for safety and learning at the University of Buffalo Boxing Club.

   1. A coach **MUST** be present at ringside during ALL "Ring Drills" and sparring sessions.

   2. Headgear, mouth guard, groin protector (males) and chest protector (females) **MUST** be worn during all "Ring Drills" and sparring sessions.

   3. You **MUST** touch gloves with your sparring partner (a sign of respect) before and after each round during all "Ring Drills" and sparring sessions.

   4. You **MUST** display good sportsmanship at all times and **NEVER** deliberately try to injure or hurt your sparring partner.

   5. Speaking and asking questions is permitted between the coach and the boxers since the "Ring Drills" and sparring sessions are essential learning experiences; however, during an actual competitive match (bout) the rule is "no talking to your opponent".

   6. No hitting below the belt.

   7. No hitting behind the head/neck.

   8. No holding onto the ropes.

   9. No elbowing.

   10. No pushing.

   Remember, the primary purpose of these "Ring Drills" and sparring sessions is to give the novice the opportunity to improve and eventually master the essential skills on offense and defense with counter punching in a controlled environment without the risk or fear of being hurt, "teach not injure".

2. **Some rules for amateur boxing**

   If you see an amateur boxing match, which is a good idea to see some matches during training, it is important that you understand some of the essential rules and procedures the boxers must follow. It is also essential to understand a few common terms used in boxing.

   The boxing match is called a "fight", a "contest" or a "bout". In an amateur boxing match, the winner is determined by the 5 judges (scoring officials) who sit at ringside. If the judges decide that the match is even and no winner is proclaimed, the match is called a draw. Each boxer is assigned a corner. One is called the RED corner and the other the BLUE corner. The other two corners in the ring are colored WHITE and are called the NEUTRAL corners. The padded section of the ropes in each corner of the ring is called the turnbuckle. Amateur boxing consists of 3 rounds lasting 2 minutes each with a 1 minute rest between rounds for the sub novice and novice division. Open class boxers fight 3, 3minute rounds. The gloves weigh 10 ounces or 12 ounces depending upon the weight class of the boxer, The 10-ounce

Part 7: Essential Rules for "Ring Drills" and Sparring

gloves are used up to and including the 141 lb. class while the 12-ounce gloves are used by the 152 lb.. boxers and above.

The officials at the site of the event, also called the venue, issue the gloves to each boxer. The referee (also called the "ref") is the person, male or female, in the ring whose job it is to safely control the match and ensure that the boxers stay within the rules. If one of the boxers is hurt during the match, the referee will give the injured boxer a "standing 8-count". This is also known as a protection count. The standing 8-count is a judgment decision made by the referee during the match. When invoked, the referee stops the action, steps in front of the injured boxer and counts to 8 after sending the other boxer to a neutral corner. The match continues if the referee determines that the match can continue safely. The referee will stop the match after the injured or hurt boxer receives 3 standing 8-counts in one round awarding the victory to the other boxer by RSC (referee stops contest). In amateur boxing, there is a "Three Knockdown Rule" which states the match must be stopped by the referee if a boxer is knocked down 3 times in the same round, awarding the victory to the boxer scoring the 3 knockdowns. Another term you may hear is "throwing in the towel". This is used when a boxer is suffering a beating, and the coach and assistants (seconds) in the boxer's corner want to stop the match (bout). They literally "throw in the towel", indicating that they are conceding the match to the other boxer.

Before the match (bout) or fight begins, the referee goes over to the boxers' corners and checks both the boxer and equipment. At this time, the referee gives directions to the boxers and says something like, "When I say stop, stop." (This means stop boxing). "When I say break, break and step back." (Meaning stop your clinch or stop holding onto each other). "When I say box, box. Protect yourself at all times."

- No hitting below the belt.
- No hitting behind the head/neck.
- No holding onto each other.
- No holding onto the ropes.
- No elbowing.
- No pushing.
- No talking to your opponent.
- If your opponent receives a standing 8-count; the boxer causing the standing 8-count **MUST** go to a neutral (white) corner
- As soon as the match (bout) is over (concluded), the doctor **MUST** immediately examine both boxers. "Good luck and come out fighting."

3. **Weight classes in Amateur USA Boxing**
   - Light Flyweight (up to 106 pounds)
   - Flyweight   (107-112)
   - Bantamweight   (113-119)
   - Featherweight   (120-125)
   - Lightweight   (126-132)
   - Light Welterweight   (133-141)
   - Welterweight   (142-152)
   - Middleweight   (153-165)
   - Light Heavyweight   (166-178)
   - Heavyweight   (179-200)
   - Super Heavyweight   (201 pounds and over)

PART 8: 100 QUIZ QUESTIONS-ANSWERS ARE FOUND IN PART 10 PAGE 127

This part includes a quiz of 100 questions based on all the essential material presented in this text and on DVD ONE and DVD TWO

Circle the most correct answer:

1. How long is the rest between rounds in amateur boxing?
    a. 30 seconds
    b. 45 seconds
    c. 60 seconds
    d. 65 seconds
    e. None of the above

2. How do you know which gloves are to be used for a match (bout)?
    a. Bring your own
    b. Use the gloves picked by your coach
    c. Use the gloves provided by officials at the arena (venue) for the match (bout)
    d. Use the gloves provided by your opponent, and your opponent uses the gloves provided by your side
        (coach)
    e. Use the gloves provided by the National Boxing Association

3. Clothing for the match (bout)
    a. Boxer has to wear a sleeveless tucked-in shirt
    b. Boxer has to wear a hometown colored shirt
    c. Boxer has to wear a long sleeve shirt matching the trunks (pants/shorts)
    d. Boxer has to wear matching trunks with the name of the team on the front of the trunks'
        (pants/shorts) lower left
    e. Boxer has to wear matching trunks with the name of the team on the back of the trunks'
        (pants/shorts) lower right.

4. Clothing for the match (bout)
    a. Boxer has to wear trunks (pants/shorts) that are just <u>below</u> the knees
    b. Boxer has to wear trunks (pants/shorts) that are tied in the back
    c. Boxer has to wear a contrasting waistband on the trunks (pants/shorts)
    d. Boxer has to wear a plaid waistband on the trunks (pants/shorts)
    e. None of the above

5. How do boxers know which corner (red or blue) they are assigned?
    a. A coin flip determines the color of the assigned corner
    b. The bout sheet determines the color of the assigned corner
    c. The referee determines the color of the assigned corner
    d. The senior judge determines the color of the assigned corner
    e. None of the above

Part 8: 100 Quiz Questions

6. If your opponent is given a standing 8 count, where do you go?
    a. You go to the blue (sad) corner
    b. You go the red (happy) corner
    c. You go nowhere. You stand still and wait for your coach's directions
    d. You go to the neutral (white) corner
    e. You go to the corner where the senior judge sits

7. Which punch sets up all other punches and combinations?
    a. The HOOK
    b. The RIGHT HOOK if you are Right-Handed
    c. The LEFT HOOK if you are Right-Handed
    d. The Left Double Hook if you are able to box with both hands
    e. None of the above

8. Which punch usually sets up all other punches and combinations?
    a. The HOOK
    b. The LEFT JAB if you are Right-Handed
    c. The LEFT JAB if you are Left-Handed
    d. The RIGHT JAB if you are Right-Handed
    e. Two of the above

9. Where would your body weight be distributed when you are in Boxing Position (your Stance or Set Position or Set)?
    a. Over your front foot
    b. Over your back foot, rear of your CENTERLINE, balanced between both feet
    c. Over your right foot if you are Left-Handed
    d. Two of the above
    e. None of the above

10. What is the difference in your power hand position when your opponent has an opposite power hand (for example, you are Right-Handed and your opponent is Left-Handed "south paw")?
    a. Your power hand moves from the side of your jaw to the front of your jaw
    b. Your power hand stays fixed below your shoulder to throw a "hay marker" when the opening exists
    c. Your power hand stays mobile below your shoulder to throw a "hay maker" when the opening exists
    d. Your power hand stays mobile just below your sternum to throw a "hay maker" when the opening exists
    e. Your power hand stays mobile protecting your sternum if your opponent decides to throw a Triple Combination of "hay maker", Power Jab, "hay maker" especially if you are winning and on the brink of victory

11. How many judges are usually present at an amateur match (bout)?
    a. 1
    b. 2
    c. 3 to 5
    d. 4 to 6
    e. more than 12

12. How many judges are usually present at a championship amateur match (bout)?
    a. 1
    b. 2
    c. 3 to 5
    d. 4 to 6
    e. more than 12

13. How many judges are usually present at a Golden Gloves championship match (bout)?
    a. 1
    b. 2
    c. 3 to 5
    d. 4 to 6
    e. more than 12

14. How many rounds are there in a standard amateur match (bout)?
    a. 2
    b. 3
    c. 4
    d. 5
    e. 6

15. How long are the longest allowable hand wraps that are used to protect hands from injury?
    a. 100 inches
    b. 120 inches
    c. 140 inches
    d. 160 inches
    e. 180 inches

16. Where does the power of your punches come from?
    a. From Einstein's equation
    b. From strong arms bulked up by weight lifting
    c. From strong arms bulked up by plyometrics
    d. From strong arms bulked up by legal steroids
    e. From application of Newton's Second Law of Motion where F=MA

17. Where does the power of your punches come from?
    a. From Newton's Equation $E=MC^2$
    b. From your body weight transfer, especially from your back foot to your front foot as in a STRAIGHT RIGHT for a Right-Handed Boxer
    c. From your body weight transfer, especially from your front foot to your back foot as in a LEFT HOOK for a Right-Handed Boxer
    d. Letters b and c are correct
    e. Letters a, b and c are correct
    f. None of the above

18. What is a good combination for the Right-Handed Boxer?
   a. A RIGHT JAB followed by a LEFT HOOK
   b. A LEFT JAB followed by a RIGHT HOOK
   c. A RIGHT JAB followed by a LEFT UPPER CUT
   d. A LEFT JAB followed by a STRAIGHT RIGHT
   e. None of the above

19. What is a good combination for the Left-Handed Boxer?
   a. A RIGHT JAB followed by a STRAIGHT LEFT
   b. A RIGHT JAB followed by a STRAIGHT RIGHT
   c. A LEFT JAB followed by a STRAIGHT RIGHT
   d. A LEFT JAB followed by a LEFT HOOK
   e. None of the above

20. What is the purpose of plyometric training?
   a. To train the fast twitch muscles for explosive power punching
   b. To train the slow twitch muscles for explosive power punching
   c. To train the ultra medium twitch muscles for explosive power punching
   d. To train the reflexes to avoid explosive power punching from your opponent e. None of the above

21. In what position should your arm be in when you throw a JAB so you can strike your opponent at the most optimal range?
   a. Your arm should be fully extended
   b. Your arm should be partially extended
   c. Your arm should be partially retracted (pulled back)
   d. Your arm should be fully retracted (pulled back)
   e. None of the above

22. What should you do after throwing your power punch?
   a. Step straight back quickly, explosively
   b. Step straight back gingerly, semi-explosively
   c. "Break" an angle to the right or left, but NEVER step straight back
   d. Two of the above are correct
   e. None of the above

23. What are some of the options you have as a Right-Handed Boxer to "break" an angle after a STRAIGHT RIGHT?
   a. "Bump" (Dip and Hop) to the right
   b. "Bump" (Dip and Dip) to the left
   c. "Bump" (Hop and Hop) to the right
   d. Two of the above are correct
   e. None of the above

24. What are some of the options you have as a Right-Handed Boxer to "break" an angle after a LEFT HOOK to the head?
    a. "Step Around" (Step and Pivot) to the left
    b. "Step Around" (Double Step) to the right
    c. "Step Around" (Triple Step) to the left
    d. "Step Around" (Triple Step) to the right
    e. None of the above

25. A basic way to quickly "break" an angle is to
    a. Pivot
    b. Duck
    c. Dip, move back explosively
    d. Two of the above are correct
    e. None of the above

26. What are some of the essential things to look for in finding a coach and a gym for training?
    a. Pick a coach who wants to find out how tough your really are
    b. Pick a coach who lets you spar with a less experienced boxer so you can improve your skills with "Ring Drills"
    c. Pick a coach who lets you spar with a more experienced boxer so you can improve your skills with "Ring Drills"
    d. Pick a coach who lets the boxers "fight it out" to see who has the heart of a champion e. None of the above

27. What is the first essential a new boxer must fully understand?
    a. Where your body weight is located so you can transfer every ounce of your body weight with every punch you throw
    b. Where your body weight is located so you can avoid your opponent's punches
    c. Where your body weight is located so you can duck explosively
    d. Where your body weight is located so you can either "Bump" or Pivot and then duck explosively e. None of the above

28. What body part usually determines where a boxer's body weight is distributed?
    a. The left arm in a Left-Handed Boxer
    b. The right arm in a Left-Handed Boxer
    c. The left arm in a Right-Handed Boxer
    d. The right arm in a Right-Handed Boxer
    e. The chin

29. What is another name for Boxing Position or Stance?
    a. Set Position or just Set
    b. "Step Around" Position
    c. "Bump" Position
    d. Letters b and c
    e. None of the above

Part 8: 100 Quiz Questions

30. What is the best Boxing Position or Stance for the Right-Handed Boxer?
    a. The left hand is open and is approximately 10-12 inches (2 fists) in front of the face just under the left eye
    b. The left hand is closed and is approximately 10-12 inches (2-4 fists) in front of the face just above the left eye
    c. The right hand is closed and is approximately 10-12 inches (2 fists) in front of the face just under the right eye
    d. Letters b and c
    e. None of the above

31. In excellent Boxing Position or Stance, the boxer's chin is:
    a. Almost always over the front foot
    b. Always rear of the boxer's CENTERLINE
    c. Always "tucked in" and is below the shoulders
    d. Letters b and c
    e. None of the above

32. In excellent Boxing Position or Stance for the Right-Handed Boxer the right hand is:
    a. Open with the thumb resting on the side of the chin
    b. Open with the thumb resting on the under side of the chin
    c. Closed with the thumb resting on the side of the chin
    d. Closed with the thumb resting on the underside of the chin
    e. None of the above

33. In the essential footwork, the fastest way to move into optimal range to throw a punch or "cut off" the ring is when the boxer
    a. Does a Pivot in any direction
    b. Does a "Double Pivot" in any direction
    c. Does a "Step-and-a-Half" in any direction
    d. Does a "Bump" (Dip and a Hop) explosively
    e. Letters a, c and d are correct

34. Which of the following is NOT considered essential footwork to be learned and mastered?
    a. The "Pivot"
    b. The "Step Around" (Step and Pivot)
    c. The "Step-and-a-Half"
    d. The "Scissor Step"
    e. The Cross Leg Step and Pivot

35. The best way to define rhythm is
    a. Rocking back and forth in Pivot Position
    b. Rocking back and forth in Step Position
    c. Rocking back and forth in Boxing Position
    d. Rocking back and forth in Dancing Position
    e. None of the above

36. The best way to define or determine range is
    a. The distance it takes for a boxer to hit the heavy bag starting from Boxing Position (Set Position), stepping forward and striking (hitting) the heavy bag with a fully extended LEFT JAB for the Right-Handed Boxer
    b. The distance it takes to hit the heavy bag with a fully extended LEFT HOOK for the Right-Handed Boxer with a Double Hop
    c. The distance it takes to hit the heavy bag with a fully extended RIGHT JAB for the Right-Handed Boxer without a Double Hop
    d. The distance it takes to hit the heavy bag with a fully extended LEFT JAB for the Left-Handed Boxer without a Double Hop or Pivot
    e. None of the above

37. The STRAIGHT RIGHT for the Right-Handed Boxer is
    a. The classic "sucker" punch
    b. The classic power or "knockout" (KO) punch
    c. The classic "square up" punch
    d. The classic "sitting up or down" leveraged punch
    e. None of the above

38. The STRAIGHT LEFT for the Left-Handed Boxer is
    a. The classic "sucker" punch
    b. The classic power or "knockout" (KO) punch
    c. The classic "square up" punch
    d. The classic "sitting up or down" leveraged punch
    e. None of the above

39. The Left-Right Combination (First Combination) is
    a. The LEFT JAB followed by a STRAIGHT RIGHT for the Right-Handed Boxer
    b. The LEFT JAB followed by a STRAIGHT RIGHT for the Left-Handed (south paw) boxer
    c. The LEFT JAB followed by a Double Right Upper Cut
    d. Letters b and c
    e. None of the above

40. After throwing the Left-Right Combination (First Combination) the Right-Handed Boxer should probably
    a. Move straight back after throwing a STRAIGHT RIGHT
    b. "Bump" (Dip and Hop) to the right
    c. "Step Around" (Step and Pivot) to the left
    d. Letters b and c
    e. None of the above

41. For the Right-Handed Boxer, the LEFT HOOK to the head is
    a. Usually thrown off the front foot shifting the body weight to the back foot
    b. Usually thrown off the back foot shifting the body weight to the front foot
    c. Usually the "Classic Arm Punch" which generates the most power
    d. Usually thrown after a Double LEFT JAB
    e. None of the above

42. As a beginning boxer (novice), what is one of the required qualities in a coach you should consider before joining a coach and a gym?
    a. The coach is usually absent during sparring sessions
    b. There is a history of competition a winning tradition and a coach who has experience teaching beginning boxers (novices)
    c. The coach who believes in a "fighting style" and with determination you should follow that approach and fight to hurt during sparring sessions
    d. The coach who believes in using the sparring sessions to primarily determine your ability to take a punch
    e. The coach who believes in a "fighting style" and with determination you should follow that approach and fight to hurt during the "Ring Drills" sessions

43. "Ring Drills"
    a. Are used by the coaching staff to teach the novice boxer both offensive and defensive skills including counter punching
    b. Are set up so an experienced boxer, along with the coach, teaches the novice without deliberately hurting the novice boxer
    c. Are used by the coaching staff to teach the novice determination by having the experienced boxer "knockout" the novice only once or twice to see what if feels like to be "knockout"
    d. Letters a and b
    e. None of the above

44. The Second Combination for the Left-Handed Boxer is
    a. A STRAIGHT RIGHT with body weight transfer followed by a LEFT HOOK to the head
    b. A STRAIGHT LEFT with body weight transfer followed by a RIGHT HOOK to the head
    c. After any Combination, the boxer should break and angle rather than stepping straight back
    d. d. Letters b and c
    e. None of the above

45. The Essential Rules of Amateur Boxing include all of the following EXCEPT
    a. No holding onto the ropes
    b. No elbowing
    c. No talking to your opponent
    d. No hitting below the belt
    e. Rabbit punches are ONLY allowed in the last round

46. The position goals for a Right-Handed Boxer boxing a Right-Handed Boxer
    a. Point your left shoulder at your opponent's chest
    b. Move either clockwise or counter-clockwise – following your opponent's movements
    c. Jab with your right hand to distract your opponent as you move to your front foot
    d. Jab with your left hand to distract your opponent as you move to your front foot
    e. e. Letters a and b

47. Defense for a Right-Handed Boxer against a Right-Handed Boxer
    a. Against a LEFT JAB, right hand block
    b. Against a STRAIGHT RIGHT, left forearm block
    c. Against a LEFT HOOK , block with back of right hand
    d. Letters a and c
    e. Letters a, b and c

48. Defense for a Right-Handed Boxer boxing against a Right-Handed Boxer might include
    a. Blocks
    b. Counter punches
    c. "Bolo" punches
    d. Letters a and b
    e. Letters a, b and c

49. Position goals if you are Right-Handed Boxer boxing a Left-Handed (south paw) Boxer
    a. Your left hand should be "outside" opponent's right hand
    b. Your left foot should be "outside" opponent's right foot
    c. Your right hand should be in front of your chin
    d. Letters a and b
    e. Letters a, b and c

50. If you are a Right-Handed Boxer boxing a Left-Handed (south paw) Boxer
    a. After your First Combination, it's best to Step Around (Step and Pivot) to the left
    b. After your First Combination, it's best to "Bump" (Dip and Hop) to the right
    c. After the Left-Handed (south paw) throws a STRAIGHT LEFT, you can block with your right hand
    d. Letters a and b
    e. Letters a and c
    f. None are correct

51. It is best to box off your back foot if you are a Right-Handed Boxer because you can transfer weight to the front foot when you throw The STRAIGHT RIGHT hand.
    a. This statement is true
    b. This statement is false
    c. This statement is true only if you are a man
    d. This statement is true only if you are a woman
    e. This statement is true only if you are a "south paw"

52. Footwork is important, but you can manage without exact footwork as long as your chin is fixed between each leg as you move.
    a. This statement is true
    b. This statement is false
    c. This statement is true only if you are a man
    d. This statement is true only if you are a woman
    e. This statement is true only if you are a "south paw"

53. All leveraged punches should be at range even when you have created an angle by either a "Step Around" to your left or with a "Bump" to your right if you are a Right-Handed Boxer.
    a. This statement is true
    b. This statement is false
    c. This statement is only true if you are a man
    d. This statement is only true if you are a woman
    e. This statement is true only if you are a "south paw"

54. Circle the correct letter:
    1. Boxing Position (Set Position) is the basic position (Stance) for a boxer
    2. A "Step-and-a-Half" is part of footwork
    3. By working the bag, you can learn range
    4. LEFT JAB, STRAIGHT RIGHT Combination is common for (Left-Handed Boxer)
    5. LEFT JAB, STRAIGHT RIGHT Combination is common for (Right-Handed Boxer)
       a. 1,2, and 3 are correct
       b. 1,2, and 4 are correct
       c. 1,2,3 and 5 are correct
       d. Only 4 is correct
       e. Only 5 is correct

55. Circle the correct letter:
    Boxing:
    1. Teaches self defense
    2. Can build confidence
    3. Is a learned skill
    4. Can still be as effective even when out of range
    5. Left-Handed Boxers have better rhythm than Right-Handed Boxers
       a. 1, 2, and 3 are correct
       b. 1,2,3, and 4 are correct
       c. 1,2,3, and 5 are correct
       d. Only 4 is correct
       e. Only 5 is correct

56. It is best to move straight back after throwing a power punch to avoid getting hit.
    a. This statement is true
    b. This statement is false
    c. This statement is only true if you are a man
    d. This statement is only true if you are a woman
    e. This statement is true only if you are a "south paw"

57. Left-Handed Boxers are called "south paws" and box with the Jab using the right hand and still box out of Boxing Position (Set Position) with the weight on their back foot.
    a. This statement is true
    b. This statement is false
    c. This statement is true only if you are a man
    d. This statement is true only is you are a woman

58. Circle the correct letter.
    The LEFT HOOK (Right-Handed Boxer)
    1. Is the hardest punch to learn
    2. For the Right-Handed Boxer is thrown off the front foot
    3. Can be effective at either Short Range or Long Range
    4. Is the third punch in the Three-Punch Combination
    5. Can be a "knockout" punch
        a. 1,2, and 3 are correct
        b. 1, 2, 3, and 4 are correct
        c. 1, 2 ,3, and 5 are correct
        d. 1, 2, 4, and 5 are correct
        e. All are correct

59. Circle the correct letter.
    The three basic punches are
    1. The Jab while still maintaining weight on your back foot
    2. The STRAIGHT LEFT (Left-Handed Boxer)
    3. The STRAIGHT RIGHT (Right-Handed Boxer)
    4. The Hook, to the head, with weight transfer from front foot to back foot
    5. The "Bolo" punch is used primarily to fool the referee
        a. 1, 2 and 3 are correct
        b. 1, 2, 3, 4 are correct
        c. 1, 2, 3, 5 are correct
        d. 2 and 3 are correct
        e. None are correct

60. Circle the correct letter.
    One of the goals of the Jab, by aiming for the opponent's eye and forehead, is to move the opponent's chin in an upward direction, which throws the opponent off balance thereby allowing you to take advantage of the situation.
    a. This statement is true
    b. This statement is false
    c. This statement is true if you are a man
    d. This statement is true if you are a woman
    e. This statement is true only if you are a "south paw"

61. Circle the correct letter.
    When fighting off the ropes, it is best to
    1. Do the Ali "Rope a Dope"
    2. Rest for a few seconds with your back against the top rope only
    3. Stay in Boxing Position (Fighting Position, Set Position, Set) with only the calf of your back leg against the lowest rope
    4. Cut off the ring first and then rest against the top rope in Boxing Position
    5. Best to fight back with "Bolo" punches off the top rope
        a. 1 and 2 are correct
        b. 1, 2 and 4 are correct

Part 8: 100 Quiz Questions

    c. 1 and 3 are correct

    d. Only 3 is correct

    e. Only 5 is correct

62. Circle the correct letter.

The purpose of "Ring Drills" is primarily to improve the skills of a beginner (novice) in the ring against an experienced boxer who will teach and not injure the beginner. a. This statement is true

    b. This statement is false.

    c. This statement is true for a man

    d. This statement is true for a woman

63. Circle the correct letter.

This purpose of "Ring Drills" is primarily to see if the beginner (novice) is able to "take a punch" and still cut off the ring.

    a. This statement is true

    b. This statement is false

    c. This statement is true for a man

    d. This statement is true for a woman

64. Circle the correct letter.

The purpose of learning how to cut off the ring is to

1. Be able to reach the ropes first (before your opponent), which prevents your opponent from "running away" from you thereby forcing confrontation (engagement in boxing)

2. Be able to reach the ropes first preventing your opponent from throwing combinations

3. Be able to reach the ropes first preventing your opponent from throwing a "Bolo" punch

4. Be able to reach the ropes first preventing your opponent from throwing a power punch

5. Be able to reach the ropes first preventing your opponent from throwing a body punch a. 1 and 2 are correct

    b. 1, 2 and 3 are correct

    c. 1, 2, 3 and 4 are correct

    d. Only 1 is correct

    e. Only 2 is correct

65. Circle the correct letter.

When you have your opponent in a corner

1. It is best to clinch and rest especially if you are tired.

2. It is best to "flush" your opponent by lunging toward your opponent's left side if your opponent is right-handed

3. It is best to "flush" your opponent by lunging toward your opponent's left side if your opponent is lefthanded

4. It is best to unnerve your opponent with "trash" talk (when the referee is not looking)

    a. Only 1 is correct

    b. Only 2 is correct

    c. Only 3 is correct

    d. Only 4 is correct

    e. None are correct

66. Circle the correct letter.
    When you are in a corner
    1. It is best to become animated, moving your head and body maintaining Boxing Position so you can still box offensively and defend yourself
    2. It is best to relax and rest for 2 seconds then spin your opponent to escape
    3. It is best to relax and rest for 2 seconds then Jab your way out to escape
    4. It is best to relax and rest for 2 seconds then grab your opponent and talk your way out
    5. It is best to relax and rest for 2 seconds then clinch and have the referee move you out of the corner a. Only 1 is correct
       b. Only 2 is correct
       c. Only 3 is correct
       d. Only 4 is correct
       e. Only 5 is correct

67. Circle the correct letter.
    If you are a Right-Handed Boxer against a Right-Handed Boxer
    1. You can counter punch
    2. You can counter punch against a LEFT JAB
    3. You can counter punch against a STRAIGHT RIGHT
    4. You can counter punch against The First Combination
    5. You can counter punch against The Second Combination
       a. 1 and 2 are correct
       b. 1, 2 and 3 are correct
       c. 1, 2, 3, and 4 are correct
       d. 1, 2, 3, 4 and 5 are correct
       e. Only 5 is correct

68. Circle the correct letter
    If you are a Right-Handed Boxer against a Right-Handed Boxer
    1. You can counter punch against a LEFT JAB after blocking with open (palm) right hand and counter punch with LEFT JAB
    2. You can counter punch against a LEFT JAB after blocking with open (palm) left hand and counter punch with RIGHT JAB
    3. You can counter punch against a LEFT JAB after blocking with open (palm) right hand and counter punch with DOUBLE SLAP SPIN
    4. You can counter punch against a LEFT JAB after blocking with open (palm) left hand and counter punch with a rabbit punch
    5. You can counter punch against a LEFT JAB after blocking with open (palm) right hand and counter punch with RIGHT DOUBLE HOOK SPIN
       a. 1, 2 and 3 are correct
       b. 1, 2 and 4 are correct
       c. 1, 3 and 4 are correct
       d. Only 1 is correct
       e. Only 5 is correct

69. Circle the correct letter.
A punch to the "solar plexus" can produce significant pain and the "solar plexus" is located
1. On your right side behind the heart
2. On your left side behind the heart
3. On your right side behind the liver
4. On your left side behind the liver
5. Just below the sternum at the pit of your stomach in the midline
   a. Only 1 is correct
   b. Only 2 is correct
   c. Only 3 is correct
   d. Only 4 is correct
   e. Only 5 is correct

70. Circle the correct letter.
A punch to the liver can produce significant pain and the liver is located
1. On your right side under the lower ribs
2. On your right side under the upper ribs
3. On your left side under the lower ribs
4. On your left side under the upper ribs
5. Just below the sternum at the pit of your stomach in the midline
   a. Only 1 is correct
   b. Only 2 is correct
   c. Only 3 is correct
   d. Only 4 is correct
   e. Only 5 is correct

71. Circle the correct letter.
If you are a Right-Handed Boxer boxing a Left-Handed Boxer
a. Your lead punch is usually a LEFT JAB
b. Your lead punch is usually a RIGHT JAB
c. Your lead punch is usually a LEFT HOOK
d. Your lead punch is usually a RIGHT HOOK
e. Your lead punch is usually a STRAIGHT LEFT

72. Circle the correct letter
If you are a Right-Handed Boxer boxing a Left-Handed Boxer
1. Your position goal is to have your left foot outside your opponent's right foot
2. Your position goal is to have your right foot outside your opponent's left foot
3. Your movement goal is to move the fight clockwise
4. Your movement goal is to move the fight counter-clockwise
5. Your movement goal is to move straight back after your combination to avoid being hit
   a. 1 and 3 are correct
   b. 1 and 4 are correct
   c. 2 and 3 are correct
   d. 2 and 4 are correct
   e. Only 5 is correct

73. Circle the correct letter
    If you are a Right-Handed Boxer boxing a Left-Handed Boxer
    1. Your position goal for your right hand is to have it in front of your chin
    2. Your position goal for your left hand is to have it in front of your chin
    3. Your position goal for your left hand is to have it outside and above your opponent's right hand
    4. Your position goal for your right hand is to have it outside your opponent's left hand
    5. Your position goal for movement is counter-clockwise
        a. 1 and 3 are correct
        b. 1, 3 and 5 are correct
        c. 2 and 4 are correct
        d. 2, 4 and 5 correct
        e. Only 5 is correct

74. Circle the correct letter.
    A punch to the head can "ring your bell" and possibly cause a concussion even if you are not "knocked out"
    a. This statement is true
    b. This statement is false
    c. This statement is true only in men
    d. This statement is true only in women

75. Circle the correct letter.
    The "floating ribs" (rib numbers 11 and 12) are not attached to the sternum.
    a. This statement is true
    b. This statement would be true if the rib numbers were 9 and 10
    c. This statement would be true if the rib numbers were 10 and 11
    d. This statement is false
    e. Rib numbers 11 and 12 are the essential ribs protecting the liver

76. Circle the correct letter.
    Abdominal exercise used to improve your core should be
    1. Performed 6 days a week
    2. Performed alternate (odd) days a week
    3. Performed alternate (even) days a week
    4. Performed so you can both "take a punch" and deliver a punch
    5. Performed whenever you wish since this is a free society
        a. Only 1 is correct
        b. 1 and 2 are correct
        c. 1 and 3 are correct
        d. 1 and 4 are correct
        e. Only 5 is correct

Part 8: 100 Quiz Questions

77. Circle the correct letter.

    In boxing, a strong core is essential for 2 main reasons: 1) so you can "take a punch", but in addition a strong core is essential 2) so you can deliver a forceful punch

    a. This statement is true
    b. This statement would be true if it did not include delivering a punch
    c. This statement is true only for men
    d. This statement is true only for women
    e. This statement is false

78. Circle the correct letter.

    In order to deliver a forceful and powerful punch, Newton's Second Law of Motion is applicable where mass (your body weight) times acceleration (the speed) equals the force of your punch. So being able to rapidly accelerate your total body weight can potentially knock a person down or even knock a person out.

    1. Therefore, by moving your body weight rapidly, you can increase your punching force (power)
    2. Plyometric training can help train you to accelerate rapidly (shoulders, arms and legs), which can increase your punching force (power)
    3. In other words, F=MA
    4. In other words, F=MAA
    5. In other words, F=MMA
        a. 1 is correct
        b. 1 and 2 are correct
        c. 1, 2 and 3 are correct
        d. 1, 2 and 4 are correct
        e. 1, 2 and 5 are correct

79. Circle the correct letter.

    In general, the rules for sparring include

    1. No hitting below the belt
    2. No "Rabbit" punches
    3. Touching gloves before and after each round
    4. The coach should usually be present
    5. The coach must always be present
        a. 1, 2 and 3 are correct
        b. 1, 2 3, and 4 are correct
        c. 1, 2, 3 and 5 are correct
        d. 1, 2 and 5 are correct
        e. Only 5 is correct

80. Circle the correct letter.

    If you are a Left-Handed Boxer boxing a Right-Handed Boxer, essentially you want

    1. The fight to go clockwise
    2. The fight to go counter-clockwise
    3. The fight to go with your coach's theory of "Bolo" punching to the neck
    4. The fight to go with your coach's theory of "Bolo" punching to the "solar plexus"
    5. The fight to go with your coach's theory of "Bolo" punching to the sternum and "floating ribs"
        a. Only 1 is correct
        b. Only 2 is correct
        c. 1 and 3 are correct
        d. 1 and 4 are correct
        e. 2 and 5 are correct

81. Circle the correct letter.
    If you are a Right-Handed Boxer boxing a Right-Handed Boxer
    1. You block a LEFT JAB with open (palm) right hand
    2. You block a LEFT JAB with open (palm) left hand
    3. You block a STRAIGHT RIGHT with left forearm
    4. You block a STRAIGHT RIGHT with right forearm
        a. Only 1 is correct
        b. Only 2 is correct
        c. 1 and 3 are correct
        d. 2 and 4 are correct
        e. Only 3 is correct

82. Circle the correct letter.
    If you are a Right-Handed Boxer boxing a Right-Handed Boxer
    1. You block a STRAIGHT RIGHT with your left forearm while turning your ankles
    2. You block a STRAIGHT RIGHT with your right forearm while turning your ankles
    3. As you block, you turn your ankles clockwise to counter punch with a STRAIGHT RIGHT
    4. As you block, you turn your ankles counter-clockwise to counter punch with a STRAIGHT RIGHT
    5. You can best block with your right elbow and counter with a double "Bolo" punch
        a. 1 and 2 are correct
        b. 2 and 3 are correct
        c. 1 and 3 are correct
        d. 1 and 4 are correct
        e. Only 5 is correct

83. Circle the correct letter.
    If you are a Right-Handed Boxer boxing a Right-Handed Boxer
    1. You block a LEFT HOOK with the back of your right hand
    2. You block a LEFT HOOK with the back of your left hand
    3. You counter a LEFT HOOK with a STRAIGHT RIGHT if you are on your back foot
    4. You counter a LEFT HOOK with a STRAIGHT RIGHT if you are on your front foot
    5. You counter a LEFT HOOK with a LEFT HOOK if you are on your front foot
        a. Only 1 is correct
        b. Only 2 is correct
        c. 1 and 3 are correct
        d. 1, 3 and 5 are correct
        e. 2, 3 and 5 are correct

84. Circle the correct letter.
    If you are a Right-Handed Boxer boxing a Left-Handed Boxer
    1. You block a RIGHT JAB with your right elbow
    2. You block a RIGHT JAB with open (palm) left hand
    3. You block a STRAIGHT LEFT with open (palm) right hand
    4. You block a STRAIGHT LEFT with open (palm) left hand
        a. Only 1 is correct
        b. Only 2 is correct
        c. 1 and 3 are correct
        d. 2 and 3 are correct
        e. Only 4 is correct

Part 8: 100 Quiz Questions

85. Circle the correct letter.

If you are a Right-Handed Boxer boxing a Left-Handed Boxer
1. You counter a STRAIGHT LEFT with a LEFT JAB after blocking with (palm) right hand
2. You counter a STRAIGHT LEFT with a DOUBLE SLAP SPIN after blocking with open (palm) right hand
3. You counter a RIGHT HOOK with a STRAIGHT RIGHT if your weight is on your back foot
4. you counter a RIGHT HOOK with a LEFT HOOK if your weight is on your front foot
   a. Only 1 is correct
   b. Only 2 is correct
   c. 1 and 3 are correct
   d. 1, 3 and 4 are correct
   e. 2, 3 and 4 are correct

86. Circle the correct letter

If you are a Right-Handed Boxer boxing a Right-Handed Boxer
1. You can switch to boxing Left-Handed any time you wish
2. You can switch to boxing Left-Handed only if you announce your intentions
3. You can switch to boxing Left-Handed only if the referee says it is okay
4. You can switch to boxing Left-Handed only in the last round if you are losing
5. You can switch to boxing Left-Handed only in the last round if you are winning
   a. Only 1 is correct
   b. Only 2 is correct
   c. 2 and 3 are correct
   d. 2, 3 and 4 are correct
   e. 2, 3 and 5 are correct

87. Circle the correct letter.

If you are a Left-Handed Boxer boxing a Right-Handed Boxer
1. You can switch to boxing Right-Handed any time you wish
2. Your best movements are to carry the fight counter-clockwise
3. Your best movements are to carry the fight clockwise
4. Best to block a LEFT HOOK with the back of your right hand
   a. Only 1 is correct
   b. Only 2 is correct
   c. Only 3 is correct
   d. 1, 2 and 4 are correct
   e. 1, 3 and 4 are correct

88. Circle the correct letter.

If you are a Left-Handed Boxer boxing a Right-Handed Boxer
1. You block a LEFT JAB with open (palm) of your right hand
2. You block a LEFT JAB with open (palm) of your left hand
3. You counter a LEFT JAB with a RIGHT JAB
4. You counter a LEFT JAB with a LEFT JAB
   a. Only 1 is correct
   b. Only 2 is correct
   c. Only 3 is correct
   d. 1 and 3 are correct
   e. 1 and 4 are correct

89. Circle the correct letter.

    If you are a Left-Handed Boxer boxing a Right-Handed Boxer
    1. You block a STRAIGHT RIGHT with open (palm) right hand
    2. You block a STRAIGHT RIGHT with open (palm) left hand
    3. You counter a STRAIGHT RIGHT with your RIGHT JAB
    4. You counter a STRAIGHT RIGHT with your LEFT JAB
    5. Your best movements are toward the neutral corners
        a. 1 and 3 are correct
        b. 2 and 3 are correct
        c. 1 and 4 are correct
        d. 2 and 4 are correct
        e. Only 5 is correct

90. Circle the correct letter.

    If you are a Left-Handed Boxer boxing a Right-Handed Boxer
    1. You block a LEFT HOOK with the back of your right hand
    2. You block a LEFT HOOK with the back of your left hand
    3. You counter a LEFT HOOK with a RIGHT HOOK if you are on your front foot
    4. You counter a LEFT HOOK with a RIGHT HOOK if you are on your back foot
    5. You counter a LEFT HOOK with a STRAIGHT LEFT if you are on your back foot
        a. Only 1 is correct
        b. Only 2 is correct
        c. 1 and 3 are correct
        d. 2 and 4 are correct
        e. 1, 3 and 5 are correct

91. Circle the correct letter.

    It is essential to know some of the anatomy of the human body.
    1. The heart is on the left side in the chest protected by the ribs
    2. The liver is on the left side in the chest protected by the ribs
    3. The liver is on the right side in the chest protected by the ribs
    4. The liver is on the right side in the abdomen (stomach) just under the ribs
    5. The heart is on the opposite side of the liver
        a. 1 and 2 are correct
        b. 1 and 3 are correct
        c. 3 and 5 are correct
        d. 4 and 5 are correct
        e. 1, 4 and 5 are correct

Part 8: 100 Quiz Questions

92. Circle the correct letter.
     If you are a Left-Handed Boxer boxing a Left-Handed Boxer
     1. Your left shoulder should be pointing at your opponent's chest
     2. Your right shoulder should be pointing at your opponent's chest
     3. You should always face your opponent with your chin tilted upwards
     4. You should always face your opponent with chin tilted upwards, if possible, since you are always in the best offensive and defensive position when you are in your Stance (Boxing Position, Fighting Position, Set Position or Set)
     5. The terms Stance, Boxing Position, Fighting Position, Set Position and Set are all interchangeable since they essentially mean the same thing
         a. Only 1 is correct
         b. Only 2 is correct
         c. Only 3 is correct
         d. 1 and 4 are correct
         e. 2 and 5 are correct

93. Circle the correct letter.
     To become an accomplished novice boxer you must **MASTER**
     1. Skills including blocks and counters against the first three punches
     2. Skills including all the essential footwork movements
     3. Skills including the first three punches
     4. Skills including the first two combinations
     5. Skills including the ability to break angles and understand range
         a. 1, 2 and 3 are correct
         b. 1, 2 and 4 are correct
         c. 1, 2 and 5 are correct
         d. 1, 2, 3 and 4 are correct
         e. All are correct

94. Circle the correct letter.
     A boxer moves to the right
     1. By pushing off the left foot
     2. By pushing off the right foot
     3. By opening and closing the Stance
     4. By opening and closing the Boxing Position
     5. By opening and closing the Set Position
         a. Only 1 is correct
         b. Only 2 is correct
         c. 1 and 3 are correct
         d. 1, 3 and 4 are correct
         e. 1, 3, 4 and 5 are correct

112

95. Circle the correct letter.
    Essential footwork includes learning
    1. "Step-and-a-Half"
    2. "Scissor Step"
    3. "Pivot"
    4. "Step Around" (Step and Pivot)
    5. "Bump" (Hop and Dip)
        a. 1, 2 and 3 are correct
        b. 1, 2, 3 and 4 are correct
        c. 2, 3, 4 and 5 are correct
        d. All are correct
        e. None are correct

96. Circle the correct letter.
    Developing or "breaking angles" include
    1. The "Pivot"
    2. The "Step Around" (Step and Pivot)
    3. The "Bump" (Dip and Hop)
    4. Allows a boxer to be in an offensive position while putting your opponent out of position
    5. Used after combinations
        a. 1, 2 and 3 are correct
        b. 1, 2, 3 and 4 are correct
        c. 2, 3, 4 and 5 are correct
        d. All are correct
        e. None are correct

97. Circle the correct letter.
    After throwing a Combination, a good move may be for
    1. A boxer to "Pivot"
    2. A boxer to "Step Around" (Step and Pivot)
    3. A boxer to "Bump" (Dip and Hop)
    4. A boxer to step straight back out of harm's way
        a. Only 1 is correct
        b. Only 2 is correct
        c. 1, 2 and 3 are correct
        d. 1, 3 and 4 are correct
        e. 2, 3 and 4 are correct

98. Circle the correct letter.
     If you are a Right-Handed Boxer, a short range LEFT HOOK
     1. Can be a "knockout" (KO) punch
     2. Left arm bent 90 degrees
     3. Left arm parallel to the floor
     4. Rapid weight transfer from front foot to back foot
     5. Thumb of left hand points toward boxer's face
         a. 1, 2 and 3 are correct
         b. 1, 2 are 4 are correct
         c. 2, 3 and 4 are correct
         d. 1, 2 3 and 4 are correct
         e. All are correct

99. Circle the correct letter.
     If you are a Left-Handed Boxer, a RIGHT JAB
     1. You "drive" off your back foot
     2. Your right arm is fully extended as the front foot lands on the floor, but your body weight is still over your back foot
     3. You exhale as you punch
     4. You inhale as you punch
     5. As your right arm retracts, your back foot slides forward back into your Stance (Boxing Position, Fighting Position, Set Position or Set)
         a. 1, 2 and 3 are correct
         b. 1, 2 and 4 are correct
         c. 1, 3 and 5 are correct
         d. 1, 4 and 5 are correct
         e. 1, 2, 3 and 5 are correct

100. Circle the correct letter.
     If you are a Right-Handed Boxer, a STRAIGHT RIGHT
     1. You "drive" off your back foot
     2. Your right arm is fully extended as the front foot lands on the floor and your body weight transfers to your front foot
     3. You exhale as you punch
     4. You inhale as you punch
     5. With your body weight on your front foot, you can throw a LEFT HOOK, transferring your weight to your back foot
         a. 1, 2 and 3 are correct
         b. 1, 2 and 4 are correct
         c. 1, 3 and 5 are correct
         d. 1, 4 and 5 are correct
         e. 1, 2, 3 and 5 are correct

PART 9: GLOSSARY

ACCIDENTAL BUTT

This is an accidental collision of heads in which the referee rules that the collision is unintentional.

AEROBIC

This is a way for an organism to produce energy using available oxygen. Aerobic exercise is an activity that increases heart rate and breathing, and this activity can be sustained many minutes or hours.

ANAEROBIC

This is a way for an organism to produce energy without using available oxygen. Boxing is mainly an anaerobic sport where you get out of breath in a few moments so training in boxing is performed at high intensity.

APRON

The part of the ring canvas outside the ropes.

ANTERIOR DELTOID MUSCLE (ALSO REFERED TO AS THE DELTS)

The deltoid muscle is one of the muscles that form the rounded contour of the shoulder.

BALL OF THE FOOT

The ball of the foot is the padded portion of the sole of the human foot between the arch and the toes on which the weight of the body rests when raising or lifting the heel. In boxing, you want to move explosively on the balls of your feet.

BEARD

Another term used to mean the chin on the face. Referring to the boxer's ability to take a punch.

BELOW THE BELT ("belt line")

An imaginary line ("belt line") from the "belly button" (navel or umbilicus) to the top of the hips. A punch below this line is a foul, and the boxer who threw the punch "below the belt" may either have points deducted by the referee or may even be disqualified by the referee.

BLOCKING

The use of the gloves, arms or shoulders to prevent a punch from landing on the intended target area.

BLUE CORNER

In a boxing ring there are two corners assigned to the boxers which are usually marked red and blue. The blue corner is arbitrarily assigned to one of the boxers and is the corner used by that boxer and team between rounds.

Part 9: Glossary

BODY BAG

A round, medium-sized bag suspended from the ceiling by ropes or chains used to practice body punches.

"BODY SHOT"

A punch delivered to an opponent's body usually in the abdomen or rib cage.

BOUT

Another name for a boxing contest or match between two boxers.

BOUT SHEET

Is a sheet of paper given to the boxers at the venue naming their opponents and assigning a corner (red or blue) for the match.

BOXER'S PASS BOOK

Is an official book provided by USA Boxing identifying the boxer by name and contains the boxer's win/loss record.

BOXING POSITION

Boxing Position is also called Stance, Set Position or Set. This term refers to the position of the boxer's arm, legs and shoulders when ready to move and punch. It also refers to the foundation or platform on which a boxer begins the process of boxing.

"BREAK AN ANGLE"

In boxing, to "break an angle" refers to changing direction. Specifically, it is changing the direction of your Stance or Boxing Position (Set Position) so you can avoid being hit while remaining in Boxing Position. The purpose of "breaking an angle" is to change direction after punching so you can throw another punch while your opponent cannot strike or hit you. The three essential angles in boxing are: 1) The "Pivot" in any direction, 2) The "Step Around" (the Step and Pivot) and 3) the "Bump" (the Step and Hop).

BREAK

The command to disengage from a referee when boxers are tangled up at a close range and cannot or will not easily free themselves.

CARBOHYDRATE LOADING

A dietary practice that increases carbohydrate reserves in muscle tissues through the consumption of extra quantities (calories) of starchy foods prior to competition to improve endurance during exercise including boxing.

CARBOHYDRATES

Any group of organic compounds that includes sugars, starches and celluloses, which serve as a major energy source in the diet of animals including humans.

CANVAS

The canvas is the floor covering of the boxing ring.

CENTERLINE.

Your CENTERLINE is an imaginary vertical line (vertical axis) starting at the top of your head extending down between your eyes and going further down between your legs. When your chin is behind your CENTERLINE your body weight is distributed or located over your back foot and conversely when your chin is in front of your CENTERLINE your body weight is distributed or located over your front foot. In your Stance, or Boxing Position, Fighting Position, Set Position or Set you want to be set to box in your unique stance with your body weight located or distributed behind your CENTERLINE over your back foot.

CLASSIFICATION (Based on experience and weight) in Amateur USA Boxing

A. Experience classes: Related to the number of bouts, "fights" or matches a boxer has had according to the classification used by USA Boxing, the official organization of Amateur Boxing in the United States of America.
1. Sub novice class – Two bouts or less
2. Novice class – Less than 6 wins and not more than 10 bouts
3. Open class – Six wins (victories) or more than 10 bouts
B. Weight classes: Related to the boxer's body weight, and the upper weight limit for each class is the lower weight limit of the next highest class.
- Light Flyweight (up to 106 pounds)
- Flyweight (107-112)
- Bantamweight (113-119)
- Featherweight (120-125)
- Lightweight (126-132)
- Light Welterweight (133-141)
- Welterweight (142-152)
- Middleweight (153-165)
- Light Heavyweight (166-178)
- Heavyweight (179-200)
- Super Heavyweight (201 pounds and over)

Part 9: Glossary

CLINCH

Both boxers hold each other and do not attempt to punch. A referee will usually order the boxers to break apart from each other quickly once it's established that neither boxer is punching effectively. It can be used as a chance to rest or for one boxer to use physical advantage in order to fatigue the opponent.

COMBINATION

A combination is a series of punches thrown in sequence.

CONDITIONING

Conditioning is performance of repeated exercises designed to build the body's strength and endurance in preparation for sports activities.

CONTRASTING WAISTBAND

The waistband of the trunks is a different color than the lower part of the trunks used in amateur boxing.

COUNTER PUNCH

A punch thrown as a reply to the opponent's punch or lead punch. Counter punching is an accepted method of offense. By drawing the opponent's lead, a good "counter puncher" can exploit openings, which appear in the opponent's defense when the lead or first punch is thrown. Hand speed, a tactical brain and timing are essential for a "counter puncher" to be effective.

CROSS

A "cross" is a punch thrown across the target with the "second" hand. Amateur boxers are taught to follow a lead punch, usually a Jab, with a cross from the other fist (i.e. LEFT JAB, right cross for the Right-Handed Boxer or RIGHT JAB, left cross for the Left-Handed Boxer.) The cross punch comes from shoulder level and is, therefore usually aimed at the head or at the upper chest of the opponent.

DISQUALIFICATION

A referee may disqualify any boxer who breaks the rules. A boxer who either refuses to obey instructions deliberately or repeatedly fouls an opponent or is guilty of serious misconduct can be disqualified by the referee and the win awarded to the other boxer. Under certain circumstances a disciplinary hearing may occur with punishment given to the offending boxer.

DOUBLE END BAG

A small bag suspended from the ceiling with a rope and attached to the floor with a bungee cord. This bag is used to teach the boxer timing--the precise moment to strike or hit the opponent. This bag is also used to teach hand eye coordination and rhythm.

DRAW

A boxing match which goes the scheduled number of rounds, ending with each boxer having an equal number of points so neither boxer wins or loses.

ERGONOMICS

Ergonomics is the scientific discipline concerned with the understanding of interactions among humans and other elements of a system and the profession that applies theory, principles, data and methods to design objects in order to optimize human performance and well-being.

EXTERNAL OBLIQUE ABDOMINAL MUSCLES (OBLIQUES)

The external oblique abdominal muscles, also just called the obliques, are situated on the sides (lateral) and in the front (anterior) part of the belly (abdomen). They are broad, thin musculature occupying the side and front wall of the belly.

FAST TWITCH MUSCLES

Fast twitch muscles are those muscles having rapid contractions associated with a high anaerobic capacity. Boxers need to train their "fast twitch" fibers of their muscles, increasing the speed of contraction; enabling quick, powerful ("explosive") movements of arms for punching and legs (footwork) for rapid position changes.

FATS

Animal or vegetable tissues made up of cells that contain fat. Examples include meat, dairy, nuts and oils that are required as part of a healthy diet.

FEINT

Basically a hand, head or body movement designed to deceive an opponent into thinking a certain punch is about to be thrown. Boxers using head, hand or body feints are less likely to be hit, while those who use the feint as a defensive tactic are also less likely to be hit.

FLOATING RIBS

Two ribs (ribs number 11 and 12) in the human rib cage. They are called floating ribs because they are not attached to the sternum (chest bone) or cartilage from the sternum but are only attached to the vertebrae (spinal column) in the back.

FOOTWORK

The manner in which the feet are used or maneuvered so the boxer may rapidly change body position is called footwork.

Part 9: Glossary

FOUL

A foul is a breach of the rules of boxing. The referee can deduct points or disqualify the offending boxer and award the victory to the other boxer.

GATE

It refers to the amount of money or receipts paid at the box office. The term "gate" was originally used in prize fighting, even if a match was held in an open field. A gate would be set up through which spectators had to pass, either paying with cash or by presenting a ticket purchased in advance. The great bare knuckle fighter of the eighteenth century, Daniel Mendoza, was one of the first to insist that boxers perform only in front of a paying audience. "Gate" can also mean the size of the crowd.

GAUZE

Bleached cotton cloth of plain weave used for bandages, dressings and hand wraps (wrapping) for competition.

GLASS JAW

A slang boxing term referring to a boxer's inability to "take" a punch and is easily "knocked out" when hit on the chin (jaw).

GLOVE TABLE

The table at the venue (the place where a boxing match is held) where officials give the amateur boxers their gloves for the upcoming competition (or match).

GOOD CHIN

A good chin is a slang boxing term referring to a boxer's ability to "take" a punch and not be easily hurt or "knocked out".

HAND/EYE COORDINATION

Good hand/eye coordination is the ability to synchronize hands and eyes together or the ability to perform tasks that involve coordinating the hands and eyes effectively to punch or hit a bag, an opponent or a baseball. In general hand/eye coordination refers to an athlete's ability to perform tasks requiring both the hands and eyes to "work" and function together.

HAYMAKER

A wild punch, usually thrown in desperation and in a sweeping motion with the aim to "knockout" the opponent.

HEAD GEAR

Head gear in boxing is a protective leather helmet-like device which covers most of the head except the face used in "Ring Drills", sparring and in amateur competition. Some head gear have nose bars for protection during training ("Ring Drills" and sparring).

HEART

The term "heart" used in boxing refers to a boxer's courage.

HEAVY BAG

A larger cylindrical bag usually suspended by chains for practicing power punches and footwork.

HEEL OF THE GLOVE

The heel of the glove is the bottom portion of the glove with rough edges, which can be used to injure an opponent. Using the glove heel is a foul and may cause loss of points or disqualification by the referee.

HITTING ON THE BREAK

Hitting on the break occurs when the referee separates clinching boxers and one boxer immediately punches the opponent without taking a mandatory step back.

HOLDING

Holding is technically a foul, but a referee will usually allow boxers to hold for a brief time if the opponent is continuing to punch with at least one free hand. Boxers hold if hurt, to conserve energy, or to disrupt the opponent's rhythm. Referees penalize this kind of holding, but will often, unofficially, use their discretion if they think a boxer is hanging on to recover. While holding, a boxer scores no points.

HOT DOGGING

"Hot dogging" is a slang term used when someone is "showing off" and generally being obnoxious.

INTENTIUAL BUTT

To use the head in a deliberate, intentional movement aimed at the opponent (usually his face). This is one of the most serious offences a boxer can commit. A referee may either deduct or disqualify the offending boxer.

JUDGE

A person who judges a boxing match.

KNOCKOUT (KO) and TKO (abbreviation for "technical knockout")

The term used when a boxer is knocked down and the referee counts to 10, and the match is over, awarding the victory to the standing boxer. A knockout may also occur if a boxer receives three standing 8 counts in a round or is unable to continue to box, awarding the victory by TKO to the standing boxer.

Part 9: Glossary

LIVER

A large organ located in the upper right-hand portion of the abdominal cavity just under the ribs on the right. It is active in the formation of certain blood proteins and in the metabolism of carbohydrates, proteins and fats.

LOW BLOW

Any punch which lands below the imaginary line across the top of the hips. The height of the boxer's trunks is irrelevant when determining a low punch. This is the referee's decision, and the referee can lower the trunks or protector of a boxer who wears them above the hip line. A "low blow" is a foul, and the boxer who threw the "low blow" (same as "below the belt") may either have points deducted or may even be disqualified by the referee, awarding the victory to the injured boxer.

MEXICAN WRAPS

Hand wraps, 180 inches in length, WITHOUT elastic (in elastic) are used during practice, "Ring Drills" and sparring sessions to wrap a boxer's hands before the gloves are applied to protect the hands, reducing the chance of injury.

MOUTHPIECE

The mouthpiece is a protective device placed in the mouth covering and protecting the teeth and gums.

MUSCLE MEMORY

Muscle memory is also known as motor learning and is a form of procedural memory that involves consolidating a specific motor task into memory through repetition. With repeated movements over time, a long-term muscle memory is created for a specific task, such as punching, eventually allowing punching to be performed without conscious effort. This process decreases the need for attention and creates maximum efficiency within the person's muscle and memory systems. In boxing, the goal of muscle memory is that all the movements, including the footwork and punches, must eventually become automatic and performed without even thinking. This process of muscle memory is achieved through practice and repetition.

NEUTRAL CORNER

In a boxing ring there are two corners assigned to the boxers usually marked red and blue, and the other two corners are neutral, not assigned to either boxer, and are marked in white.

NO CHIN

A slang boxing term referring to a boxer's inability to "take a punch" and is easily "knocked out" when hit on the chin (jaw).

NO HEART

The term "no heart" used in boxing refers to boxer's lack of courage.

NOVICE

Refers to an amateur boxer with less than 6 victories (wins) or no more than10 matches (bouts).

ON THE BUTTON

A slang boxing term referring to being punched on the full, protruding part of the point of the chin (jaw).

ON THE ROPES

A slang boxing term referring to a boxer who has been knocked against the ropes or refers to a boxer on the verge of defeat.

OPEN CLASS

Refers to a class in amateur boxing where the boxers have at least 10 matches (bouts) or less than 6 wins.

ORTHODOX BOXER

Refers to a Right-Handed Boxer or boxing as a Right-Handed Boxer.

PANIC PUNCH

Panic is a sudden sensation of fear which is so strong as to prevent logical thinking; and in boxing, a panic punch is a wild, undisciplined punch thrown in desperation.

PLYOMETRICS

(Also known as "plyos") is a type of exercise training designed to produce fast, powerful, explosive movements and improve the functions of the nervous system to improve performance in sports. Plyometrics is used to increase the speed or force of muscular contractions, providing explosiveness in a variety of sports including boxing.

PROTEIN

Proteins are fundamental components of all living cells and include many substances such as enzymes, hormones, and antibodies that are necessary for proper body functioning. They are essential to the human diet for the growth and repair of tissue. Proteins can be obtained from foods such as meat, fish, eggs and beans.

RABBIT PUNCH

A dangerous punch and a serious foul. This punch refers to the blow to the back of the neck which is the traditional country method of killing a rabbit. The referee can deduct points or disqualify the offending boxer.

RANGE

Refers to the distance at which a punch is most effectively thrown.

Part 9: Glossary

RED CORNER

In a boxing ring, there are two corners assigned to the boxers which are usually marked red and blue. The red corner is arbitrarily assigned to one of the boxers and is the corner used by that boxer and team between rounds.

REFEREE ("REF")

The referee is a person, male or female, in the ring whose job it is to control the fight and ensure that the boxers stay within the rules.

RHYTHM

In boxing, rhythm refers to movement with a uniform or patterned recurrence.

ROTATOR CUFF

The rotator cuff is an anatomy term that refers to a group of muscles and their connections (tendons) that act to stabilize the shoulder.

RSC

Abbreviation for the "referee stops contest" (RSC) because one boxer is unable to continue.

SECOND

In boxing, a second is a person who aids or helps the coach between rounds during the boxing match.

SET POSITION

Is also called Boxing Position, Stance or Set and refers to the position of the boxer's arms, legs and shoulders when ready to move and punch. It also refers to the foundation or platform on which a boxer begins the process o boxing.

SHADOW BOXING

Is an exercise of throwing punches in front of a mirror used by boxers both as a "warm-up" before other daily exercises and as an opportunity to practice and refine their foot work and punching skills.

SLAP

A punch which lands with the open glove and is not counted as a scoring point in amateur boxing.

SLIP

A slip is when a boxer falls to the ground without receiving a punch. This is not a knockdown, but a referee will normally order the standing boxer to step back while the fallen boxer rises. Before action resumes, the referee checks the boxer's condition and wipes the gloves free from any dust or debris from the canvas.

SLIPPING (PUNCHES)

Movement of the head or shoulders to avoid a punch. Punches can be avoided or "slipped" on movement forward or to the side while backward movement will usually make punches fall short.

SOLAR PLEXUS

Is a complex network of nerves located midway between the "belly button" (navel or umbilicus) and the base of the sternum (breast bone or chest bone) of the rib cage.

SOUTHPAW

Refers to a Left-Handed Boxer or boxing as a Left-Handed Boxer.

SPARRING

Non-competitive boxing in the ring at the gym where usually experienced boxers help in training younger, novice boxers. This is a valuable training opportunity where essential technical skills can be taught or improved in the ring. It should not be competitive, and none of the boxers should be injured.

SPEED BAG

Small air-filled bag anchored from the top of a rebound platform parallel to the ground. Speed bags help a boxer learn to keep his hands up, improve hand/eye coordination and help develop hand speed and rhythm.

SPLIT DECISION

Is the term used when the majority of the judges (scoring officials) vote for the same boxer and the other judge(s) scores the match in favor of the other boxer; thus, the decision is split between the judges.

STANCE

Is also called Boxing Position, Set Position or Set and refers to the position of the boxer's arms, legs and shoulders when ready to move and punch. It also refers to the foundation or platform on which a boxer begins the process of boxing.

STANDING EIGHT-COUNT

Also known as a protection count. The standing 8-count is a judgment decision made by the referee during the match. When invoked, the referee stops the action, steps in front of the injured or hurt boxer and counts to 8. The match continues if the referee determines it is safe to continue. The match will be stopped by the referee after the injured or hurt boxer receives three standing 8 counts in one round, awarding the victory to the other boxer by RSC (referee stops contest).

STERNUM

Anatomic name for the breast bone or chest bone. It is the long, flat bone in the upper portion of the chest to which the ribs are attached.

Part 9: Glossary

SUB NOVICE

Class in amateur boxing where the participants have 2 or less fights.

THREE KNOCK DOWN RULE

A rule in amateur boxing which states the match must be stopped by the referee if a boxer is knocked down 3 times in the same round, awarding the victory by TKO to the boxer scoring the 3 knockdowns.

THROWING IN THE TOWEL

When a boxer is suffering a beating and the coach and assistants (seconds) in the boxer's corner want to stop the match, they literally throw in the towel indicating that they are conceding the match to the other boxer.

TURNBUCKLE

The padded section of the ropes in each corner of the ring.

UPPER CUT BAG

Cylindrical bag suspended by ropes or chains from the ceiling parallel to the floor used to help the boxer learn to throw the punch called the upper cut.

USA BOXING

The national governing body of amateur boxing in the United States.

VASOLINE

Trademark for a brand of petroleum jelly used on boxer's face to prevent cuts when the boxer is hit in the face.

VENUE

The site or place where a boxing match or an event occurs (or takes place).

WARM-UP

A warm-up is usually performed before exercising. A warm-up generally consists of a gradual increase in intensity in physical activity (increasing your pulse rate), a joint mobility exercise and stretching of the body parts in a sport related activity. For example, jumping rope and shadow boxing warms the muscles and increases the heart rate. It is essential that warm-ups prepare the muscles physically for the required footwork and punching skills specific to boxing.

WEIGH IN

An official weighing in and measuring of the body weight of the boxers to insure they weigh within the limit stipulated for the event.

Part 10: Answers to 100 Quiz Questions

ANSWER SHEET TO 100 QUIZ QUESTIONS

1.	C	26.	C	51.	A	76.	D
2.	C	27.	A	52.	B	77.	A
3.	A	28.	E	53.	A	78.	C
4.	C	29.	A	54.	C	79.	C
5.	B	30.	A	55.	A	80.	B
6.	D	31.	D	56.	B	81.	C
7.	E	32.	A	57.	A	82.	C
8.	E	33.	E	58.	E	83.	D
9.	B	34.	E	59.	B	84.	D
10.	A	35.	C	60.	A	85.	D
11.	C	36.	A	61.	D	86.	A
12.	C	37.	B	62.	A	87.	D
13.	C	38.	B	63.	B	88.	D
14.	B	39.	A	64.	D	89.	B
15.	E	40.	B	65.	E	90.	E
16.	E	41.	A	66.	A	91.	E
17.	D	42.	B	67.	D	92.	E
18.	D	43.	D	68.	D	93.	E
19.	A	44.	E	69.	E	94.	E
20.	A	45.	E	70.	A	95.	B
21.	A	46.	E	71.	A	96.	D
22.	C	47.	E	72.	A	97.	C
23.	A	48.	D	73.	A	98.	E
24.	A	49.	E	74.	A	99.	E
25.	A	50.	E	75.	A	100.	C

PART 11: REFERENCES USED AND SUGGESTED BY COACH DEAN EOANNOU

A. BOOKS

1. Alter. Michael J. <u>Sport Stretch 2nd Edition</u>. Human Kinetics, 1990.

2. USA Boxing <u>Coaching Olympic Style Boxing</u>. I. L. Cooper, United States Amateur Boxing, Inc., 1995

3. Werner, Doug <u>Boxer's Start Up: A Beginner's Guide to Boxing</u>. Tracks Publishing, 1998.

4. Hatmaker, Mark and Warner, Douge <u>Advanced Technique, Tactics and Strategies from the Sweet Science</u> Tracks Publishing, 2004.

5. Price, Robert C. <u>The Ultimate Guide to Weight Training for Boxing, 2nd Edition</u>. Price World Enterprises 2006.

6. Frederick, Ann and Frederick, Chris <u>Stretch to Win</u>. Human Kinetics, 2006.

7. Finegan, Billy and Clark, Courtney <u>Boxing for Beginners, A Guide to Competition and Fitness</u>. Betterway Books, 2008.

B. VIDEOTAPES AND DVDS

<u>Freddy Roach Boxing DVD Set</u> Title Boxing, 2010.
www.**titleboxing.com**
1. Advanced Punching Techniques
2. Cross Training for Boxing 1 – Upper Body and Core
3. Cross Training for Boxing II – Lower Body and Trunk
4. Fundamentals of Boxing
5. How to Lose Weight Effectively for Boxing
6. How to Lose Weight Rapidly for Boxing
7. Punching Bag Training

<u>Kenny Weldon's You Can Learn to Box DVDs</u> Title Boxing, 2010. www.**titleboxing**.com
1. Basic Fundamentals
2. Roadwork/Floor Work
3. Defensive Maneuvers
4. Advanced Techniques
    a. How to Box the Slugger
    b. How to Box the Runner
    c. How to Box the Left-Hander
    d. How to Box the Fighter

Let's Rumble Video Unique Publications Video, CFW Enterprises, 1996. www.c-f-w-enterprises-inc.http
<u>Physical Conditioning for the Boxer,</u> Ringside, Incorporated, 1998. www.**ringside.com**

Part 11: References Used and Suggested by Coach Eoannou

Ringside's Great Trainers Video Series Ringside, Incorporated. www.**ringside.com**
1. Ace Miller Ringside Inc., Copyright 1997.
2. Archie Moore Ringside Inc., Copyright 1997.
3. Chris Wheless' Strength and Conditioning Video, Volume 1, Ringside Inc., Copyright 2001.
4. Istvan Javorke's Weight Training and Physical Conditioning for the Boxer Ringside Inc., Copyright 1998.
5. Jessie Reid Ringside Inc., Copyright 1998.
6. John Brown's Attacking the Body Video Ringside Inc., Copyright 2000.
7. John Brown's Counter Punching Drills Video Ringside Inc., Copyright 2001.
8. John Brown's Medicine Ball Workout Video Ringside Inc., Copyright 2000.
9. Ken Adams Ringside Inc., Copyright 1997.
10. Speed Bag Bible DVD by Alan Kahn Ringside Inc., 2009, May 22.

Wrapping Techniques by Coach Rogelio Avalos Lightfoot Production, Title Boxing, 2001. www.**titleboxing.com**

Part 12: Appendix

PART 12: APPENDIX

A. BOXING BOOKS: The 15 Must Have Boxing Books

1. Anderson, Dave <u>In the Corner: Great Boxing Trainers Talk About Their Art.</u>
2. <u>Boxing: Medical Aspects.</u> Elsevier, Apr 23, 2002
3. Collins, Nigel <u>Boxing Babylon.</u>
4. Fleischer, Nat <u>An Illustrated History of Boxing.</u>
5. Hoffer, Richard <u>A Savage Business: The Comback and Comedown of Mike Tyson.</u>
6. Job, Bertram <u>Boxing.</u>
7. Jordan, B and Herrera, J <u>Medical Aspects of Boxing (Musculoskeletal Medicine (Second Edition 2010).</u> Humana, Sept 14, 2010
8. Liebling, AJ <u>The Sweet Science.</u>
9. Mead, Chris <u>Champion Joe Lewis: A Biography.</u>
10. Remnick, David <u>King of the World: Muhammad Ali and the Rise of an American Hero.</u>
11. Roberts, James <u>The Boxing Register, New Third Edition: International Boxing Hall of Fame Official Record Book.</u>
12. Robinson, Sugar Ray <u>Sugar Ray</u>..
13. Sugar, Bert <u>100 Greatest Boxers of All Times.</u>
14. Walsh, Peter <u>Men of Steel: The Lives and Times of Boxing's Middleweight Champions.</u>
15. Weston, Stanley <u>Ring: Boxing in the 20th Century.</u>

B. COACH DEAN EOANNOU-BOXING CHAMPIONS & MEDALISTS

2017
Wendy Casey
Feliks Stamm International Tournament, Poland
Silver Medalist

2016
Kristen Mc Murtree
National Golden Gloves Silver Medalist
Kristen Mc Murtree
Upstate NY Women's Champion
Paul Hoffman
NYS Golden Gloves Champion
Tim Akeredolu
National Golden Gloves Bronze Medalist
Tim Akeredolu
NYS Golden Gloves Champion
Wendy Case
National Golden Gloves Champion
Wendy Casey
Ringside World Champion
Avery Lewis
NYS Golden Gloves Champion

2015
Wendy Casey
National Golden Gloves Silver Medalist
Tim Akeredolu
Ringside World Silver Medalist
Kristen Mc Murtree
National Golden Gloves Champion

2014
Hanna Krueger
NYS Golden Gloves Champion
Connor Smith
NYS Golden Gloves Champion

2012
Dr. Tim O'Keefe
Ringside Masters World Champion
Dr. Tim O'Keefe
NYS Masters Golden Gloves Champion

2011
Mike Christopher
NYS Golden Gloves Champion
Jack Grady
NY Western Regional Golden Gloves Champion
Paul Iya
NYS Golden Gloves Champion
Lamont Miller
NYS Golden Gloves Champion
Tim Thayer
NYS Golden Gloves Champion

NYS-New York State

2010
Mike Christopher
NY Western Regional Golden Gloves Champion
Chantell Weir
NYS Golden Gloves Champion
Sun Yung Kri
NYS Golden Gloves Champion

2009
Mike Christopher
NYS Golden Gloves Champion
John Evangalista
NYS Golden Gloves Champion
Paul Iya
NYS Golden Gloves Champion
Sun Yung Kris
NYS Golden Gloves Champion

2008
Malik Blyden
NY Western Regional Golden Gloves Champion
Wendy Casey
NYS Golden Gloves Champion
Wendy Casey
NYS Empire Games Champion
Wendy Case
Northeast Champion-Women's
Charles David
NYS Golden Gloves Champion
John Evangalist
NYS Golden Gloves Champion
Kelly Picchione
NY Western Regional Golden Gloves Champion
Chantell Weir
NYS Golden Gloves Champion

2007
Wendy Casey
NYS Golden Gloves Champion
Wendy Casey
NYS Empire Games Champion
Ian Phillips
NY Western Regional Golden Gloves Champion

2006
Carrie Acosta
NYS Golden Gloves Champion
Taylor Atkinson
NYS Golden Gloves Champion
Taylor Atkinson
NYS Empire Games Regional Champion
Wendy Casey
NYS Golden Gloves Champion
Chris Colt
NY Western Regional Golden Gloves Champion

Part 12: Appendix

SPECIAL BOXING ACHIEVEMENTS
UNIVERSITY AT BUFFALO BOXING CLUB

Voted Amateur Boxer of the Year by Buffalo Veteran Boxers Association–Ring 44

2017
Wendy Casey

2016
Kristin Mc Murtree

2015
Tim Akeredolu

2008
Wendy Casey

C. BOXING CLUBS –WEB SITES

www.boxinggyms.com
www.boxinghelp.com
www.collegeboxing.org
www.teamusa.org
www.usaamateurboxingcoaches.com
www.usaboxing.org

D. BOXING EQUIPMENT WEB SITES

www.balazsboxing.com
www.boxingconnections.com
www.boxingdepot.com
www.everlast.com
www.grantboxing.com
www.pacillo.com
www.proboxingequipment.com
www.rivalboxing.com
www.ringside.com
www.titleboxing.com
www.tko.com

E. BOXING FILMS (MOVIES)

Title	Year	Title	Year
Against the Ropes	2004	*Joe and Max*	2002
Ali	2001	*Kid Galahad*	1962
Annapolis	2006	*Kid, The*	1997
Black Cloud	2004	*Let's Do It Again*	1975
Bleed for This	2016	*Million Dollar Baby*	2004
Body and Soul	1947	*Raging Bull*	1980
Boxer, The	1997	*Real Steal*	2011
Carmen: The Champion	2001	*Requiem for a Heavyweight*	1962
Champ, The	1979	*Resurrecting the Champ*	2007
Cinderella Man	2005	*Rocky*	1976
City for Conquest	1940	*Rocky II*	1979
Creed	2015	*Rocky III*	1982
Diggstown	1992	*Rocky IV*	1985
Fat City	1972	*Rocky V*	1990
Fight Night	2008	*Rocky Balboa*	2006
Fighter, The	2010	*Rocky Marciano*	1999
Fighting Tommy Riley	2005	*Set-Up, The*	1949
Gentleman Jim	1942	*Snake Eyes*	1998
Girlfight	2000	*Somebody Up There Likes Me*	1956
Gladiator	1992	*Southpaw*	2015
Great White Hope, The	1970	*Strength and Honor*	2007
Great White Hype, The	1996	*Tough Enough*	2006
Hammer, The	2007	*Undisputed*	2002
Hands of Stone	2016	*Undisputed II: Last Man Standing*	2006
Harder They Fall, The	1956	*When We Were Kings*	1996
Hurricane, The	1999		

Part 13: Boxing Performance Tests

COACH'S EVALUATION SHEETS

BOXER'S NAME:_____START DATE:_____

	SKILLS	INITIALS OF COACH	DATE PASSED
A. Jumping Rope	1. Three 3-minute rounds		
	2. Alternate foot jumps 4, 3, 2, 1 for 3 rounds		
	3. Crisscross		
B. Hand Wraps	1. Your left and right hands		
	2. Your teammate's hands		
C. Footwork maintaining weight on back foot	1. Forward		
	2. Backward		
	3. Right		
	4. Left		
D. "Step-and-a-Half"	1. Forward		
	2. Backward		
	3. Right		
	4. Left		
E. Scissors Step	1. Quickest way for both right and left handed boxers to move to their right		
F. Angles	1. "Pivot"		
	2. "Step Around"		
	3. "Bump"		
G. Punches	1. Jab		
	2. Straight		
	3. Hook		

	SKILLS	INITIALS OF COACH	DATE PASSED
H. Combinations	1. 1st Combination-Jab, Straight		
	2. 2nd Combination-Jab, Straight, Hook		
I. Heavy bag at range for 3 rounds	**1. Dancing with the bag at range**		
	a. "Pivot		
	b. "Step Around"		
	c. "Scissors Step"		
	2. Punches at range		
	a. Jab		
	b. Straight		
	c. Jab, Straight 1st Combination-Step Around or "Bump"		
	d. Jab, Straight, Hook, 2nd Combination-Step Around		
J. Double end bag at range for 3 rounds	1. All three punches		
	2. 1st and 2nd Combinations		
	3. Footwork		
	4. Rhythm		
	5. Angles		
K. Speed Bag	1. Drills for 3 rounds		
L. Shadow Boxing all punches and Combination for 3 rounds.			
M. Conditioning	1. Stair Climbing 2. Multi-directional runs Each for 3 rounds		

Part 13: Boxing Performance Tests

RIGHT-HANDED BOXER VS. RIGHT-HANDED BOXER

	SKILLS	INITIALS OF COACH	DATE PASSED
"Ring Drills" for a RIGHT Handed Boxer	**1. Offense: vs. Right-Handed Boxer**		
	a. Position goals		
	b. Able to throw all 3 punches and both Combinations		
	c. Able to execute footwork—forward, backward, right and left		
	d. "Step-and-a-Half" forward, backward, right and left		
	e. "Scissors Step"		
	f. Angles, "Pivot", "Step Around" and "Bump"		
	2. Defense		
	a. Able to block all 3 punches and both Combinations		
	B. Blocks and counters against all 3 punches and both Combinations		
Sparring against a RIGHT Handed Boxer	1. Offense		
	2. Defense		
	3. Blocks and counter punches		
	4. Use of angles		
	5. Footwork		
	6. Conditioning		
	7. Cutting off the ring		
	8. Fighting off the ropes		
	9. Fighting out of the corner		

RIGHT-HANDED BOXER VS. LEFT-HANDED BOXER

	SKILLS	INITIALS OF COACH	DATE PASSED
"Ring Drills" for a RIGHT Handed Boxer	**1. Offense: vs. Right-Handed Boxer**		
	a. Position goals		
	b. Able to throw all 3 punches and both Combinations		
	c. Able to execute footwork—forward, backward, right and left		
	d. "Step-and-a-Half" forward, backward, right and left		
	e. "Scissors Step"		
	f. Angles, "Pivot", "Step Around" and "Bump"		
	2. Defense		
	a. Able to block all 3 punches and both Combinations		
	B. Blocks and counters against all 3 punches and both Combinations		
Sparring against a LEFT Handed Boxer	1. Offense		
	2. Defense		
	3. Blocks and counter punches		
	4. Use of angles		
	5. Footwork		
	6. Conditioning		
	7. Cutting off the ring		
	8. Fighting off the ropes		
	9. Fighting out of the corner		

Part 13: Boxing Performance Tests
LEFT-HANDED BOXER VS. RIGHT-HANDED BOXER

	SKILLS	INITIALS OF COACH	DATE PASSED
"Ring Drills" for a LEFT Handed Boxer	**1. Offense: vs. Right-Handed Boxer**		
	a. Position goals		
	b. Able to throw all 3 punches and both Combinations		
	c. Able to execute footwork—forward, backward, right and left		
	d. "Step-and-a-Half" forward, backward, right and left		
	e. "Scissors Step"		
	f. Angles, "Pivot", "Step Around" and "Bump"		
	2. Defense		
	a. Able to block all 3 punches and both Combinations		
	B. Blocks and counters against all 3 punches and both Combinations		
Sparring against a RIGHT Handed Boxer	1. Offense		
	2. Defense		
	3. Blocks and counter punches		
	4. Use of angles		
	5. Footwork		
	6. Conditioning		
	7. Cutting off the ring		
	8. Fighting off the ropes		
	9. Fighting out of the corner		

LEFT-HANDED BOXER VS. LEFT-HANDED BOXER

	SKILLS	INITIALS OF COACH	DATE PASSED
"Ring Drills" for a LEFT Handed Boxer	**1. Offense: vs. Left-Handed Boxer**		
	a. Position goals		
	b. Able to throw all 3 punches and both Combinations		
	c. Able to execute footwork—forward, backward, right and left		
	d. "Step-and-a-Half" forward, backward, right and left		
	e. "Scissors Step"		
	f. Angles, "Pivot", "Step Around" and "Bump"		
	2. Defense		
	a. Able to block all 3 punches and both Combinations		
	B. Blocks and counters against all 3 punches and both Combinations		
Sparring against a LEFT Handed Boxer	1. Offense		
	2. Defense		
	3. Blocks and counter punches		
	4. Use of angles		
	5. Footwork		
	6. Conditioning		
	7. Cutting off the ring		
	8. Fighting off the ropes		
	9. Fighting out of the corner		

Boxers MUST MASTER ALL skills with coach's approval before proceeding to
PREPARING FOR COMPETITION

VD 2 "Left-Handed oxer"

To all those who made this work possible, we say thank you; that includes the creative production work of photographer extraordinaire Marc Murphy; the insightful advice from Steve Keough; plus our loyal secretaries, Mrs. Michelle Franke and Mrs. Amy Czubja and all of our Champion boxers (listed in alphabetical order):

Ms. Wendy Casey
Mr. Mike Christopher
Mr. John Evangelista
Mr. Lamont Miller

A very special thank you to the very talented Mr. "Rugged" Robert Lewis for the video montage of some of our champion boxers and to an award-winning artist, Mr. William B. Westwood.

Finally, a giant thank you to our families for your more than generous and loving tolerance of numerous early mornings, late nights and missed weekends due to writing and rewriting and more rewriting and the endless photographic (still and video) sessions, too many hours to count; we are eternally grateful for your unwavering "knockout" support.

Coach Dean Eoannou
Eugene B. Kern, MD
Buffalo, New York
July 2014

Part 16: Concussion: Head Injury

CAUTION: Medical evidence recognizes that contact sports LIKE BOXING expose athletes to possible head injury (concussion) with potentially significant and permanent brain damage. Although head gear protection and padded gloves helps to reduce that chance of harm, those precautions do not eliminate the risk of head injury. A boxer has a duty to tell the coach or trainer if he or she has headaches, amnesia (memory loss), confusion or other SYMPTOMS of head injury (concussion). A coach or trainer has a duty to seek medical help for any boxer who appears to have a head injury (concussion) with any of the signs or symptoms listed below. It is essential that boxing coaches and trainers care for the boxer's long term health, beginning with head injury (concussion) awareness. For more information: www.cdc.gov/concussion/sports.

CONCUSSION: SYMPTOMS can be immediate or delayed for days or weeks after injury*

The most common symptoms after a traumatic brain injury (concussion) are headache, amnesia (loss of memory) and confusion; athletes MUST be cleared by the doctor before boxing again.

- Headache /head pressure

- Temporary (LESS than 1 minute) loss of consciousness with amnesia

- Confusion or feeling in a fog

- Concentration and memory complaints

- Dizziness or "seeing stars"

- Ringing in the ears

- Slurred speech

- Irritability and other personality changes

Get EMERGENCY CARE for an athlete with a Head Injury that has the following:

- Loss of consciousness lasting MORE than 1 minute

- Seizures

- Vomiting

- Headache getting worse (increased pain)

- Eye problems, including bigger pupils than normal (dilated pupils) or pupils of unequal sizes

- Changes in physical coordination, with stumbling or clumsiness

- Blood or fluid discharge from the ears

- *Concussion-text modified by Dr. Kern from the Mayo Clinic (mayoclinic.com/health)

Note: A product worth looking at is: Reebok Checklight, which monitors head injuries, see page 18, *Time Magazine*, November 11, 2013, or go to the Reebok websit

Notes

Printed in Poland
by Amazon Fulfillment
Poland Sp. z o.o., Wrocław

54902548R00085